Y0-CUX-483

New Education Can Make the World New

J.P. VASWANI

GITA PUBLISHING HOUSE
PUNE, (INDIA).
www.dadavaswanisbooks.org

Published by:
Gita Publishing House
Sadhu Vaswani Mission,
10, Sadhu Vaswani Path,
Pune -411 001, (India).
gph@sadhuvaswani.org

Second Edition

ISBN : 978-93-80743-39-4

Printed by:
Mehta Offset Pvt. Ltd.
Mehta House,
A-16, Naraina Industrial Area II,
New Delhi-110 028, (India).
info@mehtaoffset.com

ABOUT THIS BOOK.....

Dadaji is divinity embodied in human form. Having known and experienced the Truth, the Ultimate Reality, transcending the living species, genders, religions, *panthas*, languages and *samskaras*, Dadaji brings that Truth to us through his divine presence, blessings, *Satsangas*, and most importantly through his wonderful books. Annotated with everyday stories set in the contemporary context suffused with wit and humour, directly touching our heart, Dadaji's literature leads us to the path of self realization, inspiring us all the way. The practical and simple theme of these teachings is 'Service to plants and trees, birds and animals, and the poor and the downtrodden is really the true Service to God'. His life is a shining example of how God can be actually seen and realized through love and service, amidst the contradictions and challenges of modern life. Through his wonderful and easy to understand books, Dadaji brings his message that gives us hope and joy, imparting a beautiful meaning to our otherwise confused, dry and lost life.

Dr. Vijay P. Bhatkar
Founder-Executive Director
C-DAC, Pune

The World in a true sense has become a Global Village in 21st Century. It is "knowledge" that has become a unit of currency and we are witnessing knowledge linked economy. It is education that is driving force in all this vibrant and continuous change. Revered Dada has elaborated on the role of education in present scenario of knowledge linked society and knowledge driven economy in very lucid and simple language.

Dr. Arun Nigavekar
Former Chairman, UGC
Former Vice Chancellor, Pune University
Founder Director, NAAC

Dada J. P.Vaswani, who is at the head of the Sadhu Vaswani Mission, Pune, is a world renowned spiritual teacher and guide. The Mission has under its umbrella the St. Mira Schools and Colleges and Dada is at their helm. So, there is no doubt about his credentials and efficacy as an educationist.

In this book, 'New Education Can Make The World New', Dada has surpassed mere academic knowledge and excellence. Through the simplicity of his presentation, he conveys a tremendous depth and wealth of knowledge. His clarity of expression, denies and defies any ambiguity.

Dada has re-ignited the Guru-Shishya parampara, or teacher-student relationship, of ancient India. At the same time, he also provides a strong base of modern progress and technology. Dada, in his book, brings in a beautiful blend of the material and the spiritual, penetrating to the crux of true education. The core of the individual, with this education, is transformed and enlightened. Our schools and teachers should use this book as a guide and inspiration, to bring forth the students who can bring back to India its lost glory of yore.

Dr. Kiran Bedi
India's first and highest ranking woman Police Officer
and Magsaysay Award Winner

Dadaji's book on Education is written in his simple, lucid language and comes at a very appropriate time. In this book Dadaji has given in very clear language the meaning of the word education and differentiated it from literacy program by quoting not only Sadhu Vaswaniji, but several well known educationists from all over the world.

India has allotted nearly three trillion rupees for education in the current five year plan. This can be considered the second major expansion of education subsequent to the one after attaining Independence. Such large allocation of funding for education, about 22% of the plan budget, is commendable, but its optimal utilization has to be ensured so that quality education becomes accessible to everyone who needs it. The use of technology alone or expansion in the number of schools, colleges, and universities will not make the country educated.

We are witnessing many disturbing trends in our society today. The major goal of our young generation seems to be acquiring wealth by any means without regard to ethics. The acts of terrorism are occurring with increasing frequency. Divisive forces rooted in religion, language, caste, and other factors are becoming stronger by the day. The family structure and tradition are weakening. Value based holistic education is the only solution to these and many more maladies that have the potential to make the society anarchic in the long run. Unfortunately, the current education system, instead of evolving to address contemporary social needs, seems to be regressing with many gaping holes in the structure, content, and execution.

Dadaji has addressed many of these issues and pointed out how the Mira Movement was started by Sadhu Vaswaniji decades back to overcome these lacunae and spread the message of love and peace within. Sadhu Vaswaniji and later Dadaji and his colleagues have continued the same system of education for young girls realizing that educating girls will change the families and through them the nation and the world. In this book Dadaji has given simple practicable suggestions to morph the current system that merely doles out literacy, into a system that imparts education which can develop both creative and analytical parts of the brain, makes the body and mind healthy, and helps the individual grow into a complete human being with compassion for everything living.

This is a book that is a must for not only every teacher but for every thinking person to enlarge his vision and work towards self education. It is a timely and essential addition to the large number of books that Dadaji has written to bring about positive changes in our society. I consider myself privileged to have written these few words about this extraordinary book written by an extraordinary person. My sincere and humble tributes to Dadaji and I pray to the Almighty that Dadaji will continue to smile and guide generations through his gentle, yet forceful discourses, books, and interactions for a better society.

Shri A S Kolaskar
Advisor, National Knowledge Commission,
Former Vice Chancellor, Pune University

Why and how our children should be educated; what should be the content of their education; these are issues that have preoccupied some of our greatest thinkers throughout the history of civilization. Rev. Dada J. P. Vaswani's unique work on Education examines and analyses in great depth, some of these crucial issues. It is a valuable and important philosophical meditation on the whole gamut of matters relating to education.

What makes this book particularly insightful is its historical perspective, which roots education in the values and ethos of our past; at the same time, Rev. Dada brings the debate right up to the present day by engaging himself with issues and problems of contemporary education.

Much of what has gone wrong with the world today is the result of inadequate and misdirected education that alienates us from our fellow human beings in the name of competition and domination. Our youngsters begin to worry about how to make a living before they even know who they are! An undue emphasis on 'success' and high-profile careers disengages feeling from the intellect, the theoretical from the practical, the heart from the head. This only deadens the sense of wonder and joy that should be part of all learning. As Rev. Dada puts it so succinctly, "Current education has sharpened the intellect, but hardened the heart." The stress on information and memorizing only leads to inner exhaustion rather than true learning!

Education should be at its best, life-enhancing, life-enriching. Such an education will be a joyous, wonder-filled process that should be as natural as breathing fresh air! Alas, what we have today is livelihood-seeking, career-chasing education that only leaves our students stressed and strained!

The book adopts an innovative manner of presentation, adding historical anecdotes, insights from great thinkers from Socrates to Sadhu Vaswani, Aristotle to Amartya Sen, furnishing important statistical information, adding practical suggestions that are constructive and helpful, and topping it all off with a touch of humour.

Rev. Dada has indeed thrown new light on a topic that is so vital to parents and teachers and thinking people of all nations. He offers us strategies for relating educational inputs to the students' emotional intelligence, self-respect, sympathy and service-mindedness. He tackles problems like educational reform, as well as issues of accountability, equality and maintenance of standards.

I am convinced that generations of students, parents and teachers will stand to benefit from this remarkable work. In fact, I strongly feel that it should be part of the curriculum of every academic institution which seeks to incorporate value based education into its educational pattern.

Dr. (Miss) Gulshan H. Gidwani
Director, MIRA Education
Principal, St. Mira's College for Girls

Contents

1. Education: From Darkness to Light — 7
2. Education in the World: A Brief Overview — 15
3. Education in Ancient India : The Glorious Heritage of the Gurukula — 24
4. Sadhu Vaswani's Vision: The Mira Movement in Education — 38
5. What Ails Education Today? — 48
6. Women's Education — 55
7. Education: The Unfulfilled Need — 63
8. A Plea for Value Based Education — 72
9. First Pillar of New Education: Character Building — 81
10. Second Pillar of New Education: Compassion — 89
11. Third Pillar of New Education: Culture — 96
12. Fourth Pillar of New Education : Reverence For All Life — 104

EDUCATION: FROM DARKNESS TO LIGHT

Every day, early in the morning, I recite the words of the *Rishi* : *Tamaso ma jyotir gamaya!* "Out of darkness lead me into Light!"

And, I believe, the purpose of true education is even this – to lead us out of darkness into Light.

Sadhu Vaswani

What Enlightenment Does For You

There was a great Zen Master who had attained enlightenment. From being a master teacher, he had become a *bodhisattva*.

They asked him, "What were you before you attained *nirvana*? What are you now – after your enlightenment?"

The *bodhisattva* replied, "Before enlightenment, I carried water and chopped wood. After enlightenment, I carry water and chop wood."

The most important thing that enlightenment does for us is to change our perspective!

Education: From Darkness to Light

What Is Education?

Let us begin with a few known, 'text-book' definitions: at first sight, it would seem education refers to all of the following:

- the composite activities of educating or instructing; activities that impart knowledge or skill, referred to as "teaching and learning"
- the knowledge acquired by learning and instruction; what students actually learn
- the gradual process, the holistic system through which such knowledge is acquired
- the profession of teaching (especially at a school or college or university)
- the result of good upbringing, what is referred to as "breeding" or "refinement" (especially knowledge of correct social behaviour)

> **1** The central task of education is to implant a will and facility for learning. It should produce not *learned* but *learning* people. The truly human society is a learning society.
>
> *Eric Hofler*

Something to reflect on...

Many countries have a Ministry of Education; national and state governments have Departments of Education — sometimes separate Departments of Higher Education, Technical Education, Professional Education, Secondary Education, etc.

While most of us would agree that education encompasses all of the above, we would also insist that there is something less definable and tangible, something more profound involved in education: the imparting not only of knowledge, but awakening human qualities such as honesty, courage, sympathy, service, simplicity, humility, self-control, love of truth, discrimination, independent thinking, positive judgement and wisdom, etc.

And literature offers us unforgettable examples of "educated" people who must serve as warnings to us, instead of role models:

- There is Christopher Marlowe's Dr. Faustus – a Doctor of Philosophy and Theology from the same Wittenberg University that educated Martin Luther. Faustus, we are told, was so thirsty for acquiring the ultimate knowledge, that he agreed to "sell his soul to the devil" in return for occult and forbidden 'knowledge'.

- We also have Mary Shelley's Dr. Frankenstein, a scientist with an unstoppable mission, who wished to play God with his knowledge: we know he managed to 'create' a human in his laboratory, but could not control the monster he had created.

- Herman Melville created the character of Captain Ahab, who says, "All my means are sane, my motive and object mad."

We must also remember—Thomas Edison, Henry Ford, and many great entrepreneurs never really finished formal schooling. Today, every aspiring software engineer will tell you, that Bill Gates of *Microsoft* quit university to find his successful business empire.

We also have to be very clear in our minds too, about what education is *not:*

- It is not the mere-acquisition of impressive degrees like D. Litt., Ph. D., M.Phil., M.Tech., M.B.A., M.S., and so on and so forth.
- It is not filling the mind with book knowledge, statistics, facts and definitions.
- It is not just about equipping the student to earn a living.
- It is not merely sharpening the brain.
- It is not gaining mastery of certain skills or certain subjects.

> **2**
> The aim of education should be to teach us *how* to think, rather than *what* to think; to improve our minds so as to enable us to think for ourselves, than to load the memory with the thoughts of other men.
>
> ***Bill Beattie***

EDUCATION: FROM DARKNESS TO LIGHT

What is true education?

Sadhu Vaswani said, "Education is essentially a thing of the Spirit."

If education does not lead us from the darkness of fear, prejudice, greed and ignorance into the light of peace, joy, serenity, compassion, humanism, faith and love for all creation, then it is not true education at all!

Harvard, Stanford, Oxford, Cambridge, the IITs and IIMs can give us degrees and diplomas; but these will remain paper qualifications, if we have not acquired the art of living a worthwhile, meaningful life, somewhere along the way!

The provision of universal and compulsory education for all children in the age group of 6-14 was a cherished national ideal and had been given overriding priority by incorporation as a Directive Policy in Article 45 of the Constitution. It is only in 2010, that this is beginning to be implemented.

> **3** It is possible to store the mind with a million facts and still be entirely uneducated.
>
> *Alec Bourne*

FACT FILE

Did You Know?

- The Right to Education is a fundamental human right. UNESCO aims at education for all by 2015. India is one of the countries (along with the Arab states and sub-Saharan Africa) where the literacy levels are still below the threshold level of 75%.

- India accounts for 20% of the world's out-of-school children and 35% of adult illiterates.

- In his book *The Argumentative Indian*, Amartya Sen notes, on the basis of investigations by Pratichi Trust, set up with the proceeds of his Nobel award, carried out in West Bengal and Jharkhand, that absenteeism of comparatively well-paid teachers, particularly where bulk of the students come from scheduled castes and tribes, poses a major problem.

- Between 2005-06 and 2017-18, the number of bachelor's degrees is projected to increase 16% overall; increase 15% for men; and increase 18% for women.

NEW EDUCATION CAN MAKE THE WORLD NEW

- The total number of elementary and secondary teachers increased 27% between 1992 and 2005 and is projected to increase an additional 18% between 2005 and 2017.

- The US researchers tell us that among youth ages 5–18, there were 17 school-associated violent deaths from July 1, 2005, through June 30, 2006 (14 homicides and 3 suicides). In 2005, among students' ages 12–18, there were about 1.5 million victims of nonfatal crimes at school, including 868,100 thefts and 628,200 violent crimes.

—*The National Center for Education Statistics (NCES), USA*

4
Education is what survives when what has been learned has been forgotten.

B. F. Skinner

5
Education... has produced a vast population able to read but unable to distinguish what is worth reading.

G. M. Trevelyan

What education can do for us...

- Cultivate our character.
- Help us to grow in the spirit of reverence for what is above us, around us and beneath us.
- Make us learners for life.
- Help us to choose the right means in a competitive world.
- To grow in the spirit of living not for self alone but also for others.
- Make God the centre of our life.
- Make us sensitive, compassionate human beings.
- Help us to take responsibility of our own life and our doings.
- Help us develop analytical and critical abilities to become good decision makers.
- Inculcate moral and ethical values in us.
- Enable us to appreciate the value of physical well being and fitness.
- Foster appreciation for our cultural heritage.
- Develop our creative abilities.
- Remind us of the first and most essential truth of this human life: that we have been born for a purpose; and to enable us to fulfil that purpose.
- Strengthen our awareness of the Spirit within, the *Atman*, and never to do anything that will diminish its effulgence.
- Purify our heart and help us grow in perfection.

EDUCATION: FROM DARKNESS TO LIGHT

YUDISHTHIRA'S EDUCATION:

As young students, the five Pandava brothers – Yudishthira, Bhima, Arjuna, Nakula and Sahadeva were sent to a Gurukula for their education. On the first day, the very first lesson that the *rishis* taught them was, *"Satyam Vadha, Krodham Makuru."* Always speak the truth, never yield to anger. The following day, their guru asked them, "Did you learn yesterday's lesson?" Bhima, Arjuna, Nakula and Sahadeva replied, "Yes, we learnt the lesson." Yudishthira was an exception. He said, "I have learnt only the first half – *Satyam Vadha."*

"This child must be a dullard," the guru said to himself. "How can he not learn such a simple lesson?" He instructed him to learn the second part that day.

The following day, he asked him again, "Have you learnt the full lesson?"

Yudishthira gave him the same response. This pattern repeated itself for the next five days.

On the sixth day, when Yudishthira said that he had only learnt half the lesson, the guru lost his temper. "Are you a dud? Have you no brains, you good-for-nothing boy? You are the eldest amongst your brothers! What will you do when you grow up? Can you not learn a simple lesson?"

After the teacher had said all that he had to say, Yudishthira said, "Now I have learnt the whole lesson."

> **6** Education is the manifestation of the perfection already in man.
>
> *Swami Vivekananda*

13

The guru was shocked. "What is this? Your words are a mystery to me," he said.

Calmly Yudishthira answered, "The first part — always speak the truth — was easy to learn. But I was not sure I had learnt the second part. No one had ever been really angry with me; how could I say that I had controlled my temper? It is only when you became angry now, that I realised that my mind was at peace and that I did not wish to retaliate. Now, I can honestly say that I have learnt the full lesson."

In A Lighter Vein...

At a dinner held in his honour one evening, the President of Harvard University, Charles W. Eliot, was being felicitated with toasts from several of his learned professors. "Since you became the president of our university," one of them gushed, "Harvard has become a storehouse of knowledge."

"What you say is true, but I can claim little credit for it," Eliot replied. "It is simply that the freshmen bring so much in and the seniors take so little away!"

EDUCATION IN THE WORLD: A BRIEF OVERVIEW

Education must not be merely academic or abstract. It must not merely aim at stuffing the students with information acquired from dead books or a set of sterile moralities and superficial values.

True education should equip the students to cope adequately with life, with what lies ahead of them so that they may become worthy participants in the adventure of life.

J. P. Vaswani

WHOSE MONEY?

Chris Whittle was an American education entrepreneur, and the founder and CEO of Edison Schools. He often had to use all his charm and missionary zeal to raise funds to finance a firm which, he claimed, would tackle and privatise America's beleauguered school system.

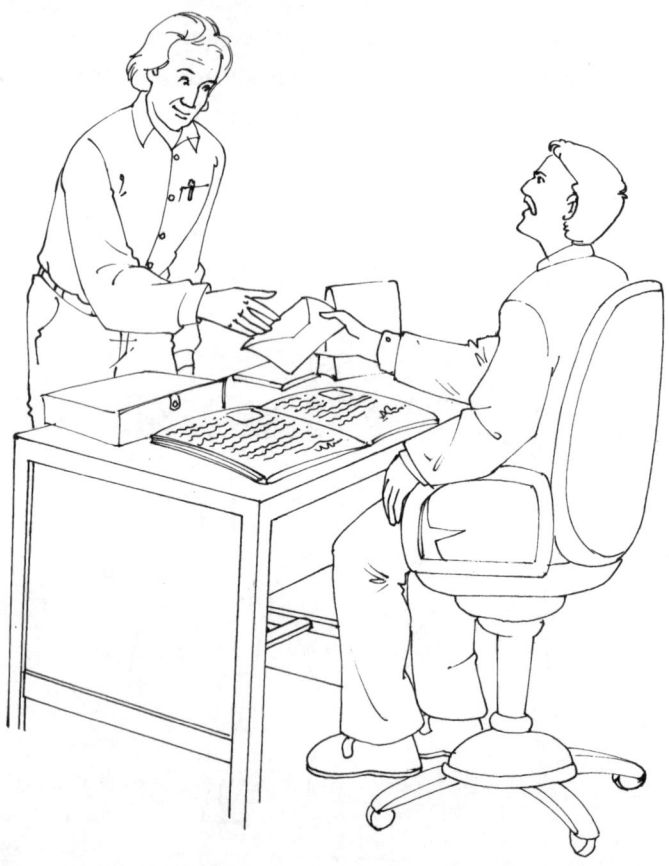

One day, he was in a meeting with a very well-known American capitalist, trying to get a donation from the millionaire. During the meeting, the millionaire remarked, "God, what dirty work!"

EDUCATION IN THE WORLD: A BRIEF OVERVIEW

Chris Whittle was taken aback. He said, "What do you mean?" And the millionaire said, "All those parents calling you all the time!" What he actually meant was that it was a tough job, trying to raise funds for education.

And then as Whittle was walking out of the room, he tried one last ploy: "You know, there's another reason you ought to donate your money for this cause." The millionaire was intrigued. He said, "What's that?" Whittle replied, "It's God's work." The millionaire replied, "True, but it's not God's money!"

Education in the World: A Brief Overview

This chapter must necessarily open with a disclaimer: I am no historian; nor am I a social scientist. My interest in education and allied matters arises from this one view of mine – that I consider myself a humble student, a learner in the vast school of life. The day on which I have learnt nothing new, I consider a lost day indeed.

But I must emphasise that the historical perspective, the world perspective is essential for us. Today, India is one of the leading providers of education in the world. As recently as twenty years ago, our young men and women thought it the height of their ambition to study abroad and acquire a 'foreign' degree. I hardly need to tell you, that today, there is a reversal of this trend; thousands upon thousands of foreign students are arriving in India every year to pursue degrees in the Arts, Sciences, Vocational Courses, Agriculture, Engineering, Ancient Languages and so on! The wheel has come full circle, with a reverse brain-drain of our own people, who now find the Indian Education scene vibrant and alive.

There is yet another reason why I choose to focus on the historical perspective: that is, to pay tribute to some of those great forces, the unquenchable aspiration of the early forebearers of human civilisation, who helped to shape modern education as we know it today.

- Education in an informal mode, must have existed since the dawn of civilisation – for man has always been a learning animal! Apart from hunting, gathering and farming, the ancient communities must surely have passed on their values, beliefs and customs to the generations that succeeded. Thus man reaped the benefits of
  – agriculture
  – domestication
  – settlement
  – a refined diet that included vegetables and cereals
  – building
  – trading

EDUCATION IN THE WORLD: A BRIEF OVERVIEW

- barter and exchange
- development of new skills and methods

All of the above, remarkably enough, was achieved largely through *oral* tradition!

- It is thought that writing systems began to evolve around 3500 B.C. This, as we can imagine, would accelerate the process of passing and sharing of knowledge within a community and between different societies.

- It is thought that men and boys must have taken to formal learning skills, crafts, trades and weaponry, while girls would have learnt housekeeping and cooking from their mothers.

- Much has been discovered about the ancient learning systems of Mesopotamia, Sumeria, Egypt and the Indus Valley. The first library of ancient Cuneiform texts was established in Nineveh.

- In ancient Egypt, the Hieroglyph system of picture writing was made deliberately more difficult – so as to preserve the elite status of scribes who could write.

- In contrast, basic education was widespread in ancient Judah (modern Israel) because the Hebrew scriptures commanded all Jews to read, learn, teach and write the *Torah*. The expense for such education was borne by the community.

- In India, we had the Gurukul system of education, which formed the basis of Hindu education. [To this a separate chapter is devoted in the following pages.]

- Ancient China too, depended on literate, educated men to help govern the vast empire. It is said that the Zhou dynasty even developed a formal system of examination and evaluation to select the best men for taking up office as

NEW EDUCATION CAN MAKE THE WORLD NEW

administrators. This was perhaps the oldest merit-based system of selection. It was this era that gave rise to Chinese philosophy which we still respect today – the teachings of Confucius and Lao Tse.

- In ancient Athens were established the finest and best academies in Europe, for teaching the Liberal Arts, Science, Mathematics, Politics, Ethics and Metaphysics. It was Athens which gave us the great teacher-student trio – Socrates, Plato and Aristotle.

- Higher Education in the Roman Empire was more of a status symbol. But great Masters like Quintilian recognised the importance of early education, with an emphasis on cultivating "the gift of learning".

- Perhaps the world's oldest centres of Higher Education were the ancient Indian Universities of Nalanda and Takshashila, Ujjain and Vikramshila. Art, Architecture, Painting, Logic, Mathematics, Grammar, Astronomy, Literature, *Arthashastra* (Economics) were all taught here – on the basis of ancient Hindu scriptures like the Vedas and the Upanishads. Takshashila specialised in Medicine, Ujjain emphasised Astronomy, while Nalanda handled all branches of known knowledge including the teaching of Hinduism, Buddhism and Jainism.

- With the advent of Islam, religious education was taken up with great zeal in the Arab region. Though religion and learning were at first centred in the mosque, by the 9th century A.D., *madrasas* were established. Philosophers like al-Kindi and al-Farabi translated the works of Aristotle and applied his theories to Islamic philosophy.

- In Japan, learning and education came largely through Chinese influence, and Zen Buddhist monasteries were centres of learning.

- In early Christian Europe, the church dominated higher education, which was only available through the classical languages – Greek and Latin. Theology dominated all learning, and the early Greek influences on a liberal, universal, humanistic learning, were kept at bay.

- It was Emperor Charlemagne of France who brought about a flowering of scholarship in Literature, Arts and Architecture in the 9th century A.D. He also promoted the study of Grammar, Rhetoric, Arithmetic and Astronomy.

- In the 11th and 12th centuries, Universities were established in several European cities. The Renaissance brought scholarship to a wide population, promoting scholarship in literature, philosophy, music and arts.

EDUCATION IN THE WORLD: A BRIEF OVERVIEW

HISTORY TELLS US...

- In the Aztec kingdom (Mexico), education was mandatory for all children, regardless of gender, rank and station.

- Education among the Incas of South America was socially discriminatory, with aristocrats receiving formal education, while ordinary people learnt knowledge and skills from their fathers. Girls were not taught to read or write.

- 17th Century Europe witnessed the setting up of Universal education promulgated by educationist and scientist *John Amos Comenius*. This led to increased government involvement in education.

- The first chair of Pedagogy was established at the University of Halle in Germany, in the 1770s. Pestalozzi of Switzerland and Joseph Lancaster of Britain were the educational thinkers of this period.

- Berlin University, founded in 1810, became the model for Research Universities.

- By the late 19th century, universal elementary education was widespread in Europe.

- In the 20th century, primary education received a tremendous, transformational boost through the work of Maria Montessori.

- Jules Ferry, Minister of Public Instruction in France, created the modern *Republican* school, where education was free of charge for all students.

- In America, wealthy philanthropists helped to establish world class universities with the aim of providing a truly wide range of education. Millionaires like Harvard, Wharton, Stanford and Carnegie are

remembered today by the great universities that they helped to establish. We can cite the inscription that is still to be found in one of America's well-known universities: "I would fain found an institution where any man can receive instruction upon any subject." America's greatest contribution to world education was what is now referred to as democratisation of the curriculum.

- The Communist Revolution in Russia created the socialist system of education, with abolition of illiteracy proclaimed as the primary aim. Thus Universal compulsory education was established for all children.

- In Africa, until the early 20th century, children received informal, traditional education, which included training in artistic performances, singing, dancing and rituals. Boys and girls were educated separately, to prepare them for their adult life. Such was the influence of this informal system, that formal education never really took off in Sub-Saharan Africa, till late in the 20th century.

Today, many of the world's nations have been tackling the problem of illiteracy successfully.

Did you know?

- The UN has proclaimed the right to education as a fundamental human right. The European Convention on Human Rights obliges all signatories to guarantee the right to education.

- Recent trends include Alternative Education, designed for students with special needs, employing alternative educational methods and philosophies.

- Technology has now become an important aspect of education. Computers, Multimedia, Virtual learning and Online Education have become increasingly popular. Information and Communication Technology (ICT) is all set to revolutionise education, in both developed and developing countries.

> **7** To govern well is to train up a nation in true wisdom and virtue, and that which springs from thence, magnanimity.
>
> *John Milton*

In a Lighter Vein...

Peter Ustinov once received a letter from the headmaster of his young son's school. The boy had assumed the unfortunate role of class clown, the master explained. Moreover, his antics made classmates laugh and were a distraction. Could Ustinov not control the child?

Ustinov's reply was prompt. He was able to afford the school's high fees, he declared, only because he was well compensated for assuming very similar roles in his movies.

EDUCATION IN ANCIENT INDIA : THE GLORIOUS HERITAGE...

What constitutes a school? Emphasis is often put upon building or furniture. But the school, as I think of it, is not the place, but the atmosphere that the teachers and students move in. Fellowship of teachers and students – that is what makes the school. So it was in ancient India. The centre of the school – the *ashrama* – was the guru, whereby was meant not a pedagogue, but a teacher who carried with him a purifying atmosphere.

Sadhu Vaswani

EDUCATION IN ANCIENT INDIA : THE GLORIOUS HERITAGE...

SATYAKAMA

One day a young boy came to Sage Gautama's *ashrama* and said, "*Rishivar*, I humbly seek to gain sacred knowledge by serving you. Pray accept me as your disciple."

The sage asked, "Child, What is your *gotra?*" (i.e. family name).

The boy replied, "Sire, my mother could not tell me my *gotra*. All she said to me was, "My name is Jabala and yours, Satyakama. So call yourself Satyakama - Jabala and give this as your name to the Guru."

On hearing it, the *rishi* smiled and said, "I am pleased with you, dear child, for speaking the truth. I shall accept you as my student."

Satyakama was initiated into *brahmacharya* by the Guru, and accepted in the *gurukul*.

After a few days, the *rishi* called the young boy to him. He was given four hundred lean and ill fed cattle and the Guru said to him, "Child, take these to the forest and graze them. You shall return to my *ashrama* when you think the time is right."

Satyakama bowed to the Guru and said, "Sire, I shall return when these cows multiply into a thousand."

Satyakama built an *ashrama* for himself in the forest and led the life of a simple cowherd, grazing the cows. All this while, he carefully adhered to the prescribed duties of a *brahmachari*.

25

NEW EDUCATION CAN MAKE THE WORLD NEW

Years went by. The number of cows increased to a thousand.

One day a bull among them spoke to him, "Satyakama! Now the cows are a thousand in number. Take them to your Guru. I shall teach you one-fourth of the sacred truth about *Brahman* or God. His name is *Prakasavan*." And he taught Satyakama a quarter of the sacred truth.

Satyakama thought it was time he returned to the *gurukula*. Accordingly, he drove the cows to the Guru's *ashrama*.

He stopped on the way for the night and lighted a fire to warm himself.

From that fire Lord Agni appeared before him and said, "Satyakama! I shall teach you the second quarter of the sacred truth about *Brahman*. He is called *Anantavan*."

On the following evening Satyakama stayed near a lake along with the cows.

At that time a swan came flying from the waters and said, "Satyakama! I shall teach you the third quarter of the truth about *Brahman*. He is called *Jyotishman*."

On the following day, he stayed beneath a peepal tree.

In the evening a waterfowl came before him and said, "Satyakama! I shall teach you the fourth and last part of *Brahman*. He is called *Ayatanavan*."

On the following day, Satyakama reached the Guru's *ashrama* with the thousand cows. The Guru saw that his face was shining with a divine radiance. "Dear Satyakama," he said, "I can see from the radiance on your face, that you are a *Brahmagyani*. How did you come by this sacred knowledge?"

Satyakama told him about his four teachers and said, "Sire, I humbly request you to teach me *Brahma Gyana* personally. Your grace alone can make my knowledge perfect."

The *rishi* said, "Child! You have been blessed with true *Brahma Gyana*. There is little else that I can add to your knowledge. I bless you!"

By obeying and serving the Guru faithfully, Satyakama attained true spiritual knowledge.

Education in Ancient India: The Glorious Heritage of the Gurukula

Hindu children are the inheritors of one of the greatest cultural, religious and spiritual traditions of the world. However, many Hindu children in affluent Western and Westernised societies are unaware of their priceless heritage.

This great heritage was preserved for us through the devotion and commitment of the *rishis* and sages, in their *gurukulas* or *ashramas*. The word *kula* means 'family'. *Gurukula* thus refers to the Guru's family or the Guru's household. In ancient India, the Gurus lived in *ashramas* or forest hermitages, where disciples came to live with them, serve them, and imbibe knowledge at their feet. Just as children at home learn everything from living with their parents and observing their behaviour, the disciples at the *gurukula* were like spiritual children, learning by close contact and observation. Thus the *gurukula* offered much more than academic teaching: it offered a holistic and integral education of body, mind and spirit. But this life of simplicity and service was for the disciple's own benefit and inner growth. You could say that India's *gurukula ashramas* were perhaps the world's earliest residential schools!

Ancient was the *gurukula* tradition. We saw from the story of Satyakama, that it is mentioned in the Upanishads. We know too, that Sri Rama and Sri Krishna, benefited from this great system of education in their youth.

The *Gurukula* system of education supported traditional Hindu learning; the *ashrama* was typically the teacher's house or a monastery, often located in pleasant green, natural environs. Education was free, but students from well-to-do families paid *Gurudakshina*, a voluntary contribution after the completion of their studies. At the *Gurukula*, the teacher imparted knowledge of *Sanatana dharma*, the sacred Vedic Scriptures, as well as Philosophy, Literature, Warfare, Statecraft, Medicine, Astrology and History.

EDUCATION IN ANCIENT INDIA : THE GLORIOUS HERITAGE...

In ancient India, a *shishu* or a *shishya* was referred to as a disciple in the Guru's *ashrama*. According to the Hindu *Dharma*, life was divided into the four stages of *Brahmacharya* (literally, 'one who walks with God' i.e. the stage of childhood and celibate youth), *Grihasta* (householder), *Vanaprastha* (householder who has begun his quest for spiritual pursuits) and *Sanyasin* (a person who gives up wordly attachments in search of spiritual quest). In the first stage of *Brahmacharya*, Hindu children were sent to the *ashramas* and *gurukulas* where traditional Vedic education was imparted to them, not through book learning or lecturing, but by a combination of *Shruti* (hearing), *Smriti* (memorising) and *sloka-pathan* (recitation).

Here is what the Vedas tell us about the *Bramhacharya* stage:

The first stage of life (up to the age of 25) covers the period of study, when a student cultivates his mind and prepares himself for future service to society. He lives with his teacher and regards his teacher as his spiritual father. He leads an austere life and conserves his energy, spurning the defilement of the body and mind through evil words, thoughts and deeds. He shows respect to his elders and teachers, and becomes acquainted with the cultural achievements of the race. Students, rich and poor, live under the same roof and receive the same attention from the teacher and his wife. When the studies are completed, the teacher gives the pupil the following instructions, as described in the Taittiriya Upanishad:

Speak the truth. Practice Dharma. Having brought to the teacher the gift desired by him, enter the householder's life and see that the line of progeny is not cut off. Do not swerve from the truth. Do not swerve from Dharma (path of Virtue). Do not neglect personal welfare. Do not neglect prosperity. Do not neglect the study and teaching of the Vedas. Do not neglect your duties to the Gods and the Manes. Treat (revere) your mother as Goddess. Treat your father as God. Treat your teacher as God. Treat your guest as God.

Whatever deeds are faultless, these are to be performed - not others. Whatever good works have been performed by us, those should be performed by you – not others.

Sanskrit was the language of learning. The education system involved three basic processes which included '*Sravana*', '*Manana*' and '*Nididhyasana*'.

- In the first stage *sravana* (listening) students received knowledge orally and it was passed on from generation to generation.

- The second stage was *manana* which means the pupils had to think for themselves and make inferences and assimilate the lesson.

- The third stage was *nididhyasana* means complete understanding and internalisation of the lesson.

Maharishi Vyasa tells us the conduct expected of the *brahmachari* in the *gurukula*:

For the (first) fourth part of his life, the brahmachari, conversant with the distinctions of duty and freed from malice, should live with his preceptor or his preceptor's son. While residing in the preceptor's house, he should go to bed after the preceptor has gone to his, and rise therefrom before the preceptor rises from his.

All such acts again as should be done by the disciple, as also those which should be done by a servant, should be accomplished by him. Finishing these he should humbly take his stand by the side of the preceptor. Skilled in every kind of work, he should conduct himself like a servant, doing every act for his preceptor. Having accomplished all acts, he should study, sitting at the feet of his preceptor, with eager desire to learn. He should always behave with simplicity, avoid evil speech, and take lessons only when his preceptor invites him for it.

He should never eat before his preceptor has eaten; never drink before his preceptor has drunk; never sit down before his preceptor has sat down; and never go to bed before his preceptor has gone to bed. He should gently touch his preceptor's feet with upturned palms, the right foot with the right and the left with the left. Reverentially saluting the preceptor, he should say unto him, 'O illustrious one, teach me. I shall accomplish this (work), O illustrious one! This (other work) I have already accomplished. O regenerate one, I am ready to accomplish whatever thy reverend self may be pleased to command.'

...This is consistent with the ordinance. Whatever observances have been elaborately laid down for Brahmacharis (in the scriptures) should all be regularly practised by him. He should, again, be always near his preceptor (ready within call). Having contributed to his preceptor's gratification in this way to the best of his powers, the disciple should, from that mode of life, pass into the others, one after the other.

From the translation by Sri Kisari Mohan Ganguli

EDUCATION IN ANCIENT INDIA : THE GLORIOUS HERITAGE...

The Unclean Vessel

There was an aspirant who went to a saint and announced that he had chosen the saint as his Guru. He fell at the Guru's feet and said to him, "Now that I have become your disciple, kindly give me enlightenment."

The Guru said to him, "Come and live in my *ashrama*; follow the *sadhana* and austerities that we practise here; by and by, I will begin to impart my teachings to you."

However, the aspirant was impatient. "O Sire, I know you are an enlightened soul," he said. "As for me, I am determined to attain enlightenment. Why should I waste time, joining the *ashrama* and following the routine of the other disciples and so on? I am not really interested in

sadhana and austerities. My one and only goal is enlightenment. I know you can give it to me with your *taposhakti*. So why don't we dispense with all the formalities and get on with my enlightenment?"

The Guru smiled inwardly at the ignorance of the aspirant. But he said to the *shishya*, "I will give the answer to your question when I come to receive *biksha* at your residence. Tell me when you are ready to receive me."

The aspirant was overjoyed. "I am deeply honoured, *Gurudeva*," he said. "I cordially invite you to visit my home next Friday, when it will be my privilege to offer you *biksha*."

"Next Friday?" said the Guru. "Why wait that long? Today or tomorrow would suit me fine!"

"But Sire," protested the disciple, "it is not everyday that a saint of your stature and eminence comes to my house to accept my hospitality! For me and my family, this is a rare and prestigious opportunity. We shall spare no effort to make this event a memorable occasion. And then, my neighbours and business associates must be informed, too. I will want everyone I know to be present at my mansion to witness this wonderful visit. Further, I come from a rich and powerful family which is known for its munificence and lavish hospitality. I cannot bring down the family prestige by offering you poor hospitality. Do pray take all this into consideration, and allow me time till next Friday, so that I may entertain you in a manner that befits your holiness and my station in life."

"As you wish," was the Guru's reply.

On the appointed day, the Guru walked to the man's house, carrying his begging bowl. He was received by an array of musicians, temple priests and guests and ceremoniously escorted to a grandly decorated banquet hall, where a seat of honour had been prepared for him. Servants bearing delicious dishes waited to serve him, the moment he was seated.

The Guru took his seat and placed his begging bowl before him, pushing aside the solid silver dinner-plate that had been placed there. "Put into this bowl whatever you have to offer me," he said to his host.

The aspirant was taken aback. "But *Gurudeva*," he protested, "I have ordered the most exclusive, the most exotic and the most expensive delicacies to be prepared for you. How can we dump it all inside this bowl?" He peered gingerly into the bowl and added, "And this bowl, with due respect, is not even clean!"

"Surely you know that a renunciate like me can only eat out of my begging bowl," the Guru replied. "So let the food be served in it."

"At least permit me to wash this bowl thoroughly" begged the disciple.

"There's no need for such needless rituals," the Guru insisted. "Come, put the food in here."

"But that's not fair," cried the aspirant. "Why Sire, you seem bent on insulting my hospitality. Do you think the delicious dishes we have prepared for you are fit only to be dumped into an unclean bowl? Is this the regard you show to one who has spared no pains to offer you the best?"

"Why, look now son, how reluctant you are to serve food in my bowl, because you consider it to be an unfit, undeserving receptacle for the rich dishes you have prepared," the Guru said to him. "But you did not pause to consider whether you were fit and ready and deserving to receive the best teachings that I could give you! You were unfit, unprepared, impure and unclean – and you would not go through the process of preparation and purification. How is your food superior to the enlightenment you sought at my hands?"

The aspirant bowed his head in shame.

> **8** Always attending to the Vedas, silently reciting the mantras obtained from his preceptor, worshipping all the deities, O Yudhishthira, dutifully waiting upon and serving his preceptor with his own body, the person leading the *Brahmacharya* mode of life should always observe rigid vows and, with senses under control, should always pay attention to the instructions he has received. Reflecting on the Vedas and discharging all the duties, he should live, dutifully waiting upon his preceptor and always bowing unto him. Unengaged in the six kinds of work, and never engaged with attachment to any kind of acts, never showing favour or disfavour to any one, doing good even unto his enemies, these, O sire, are the duties laid down for a *Brahmacharin!*
>
> *–Bhishmacharya, speaking to Yudhishthira, in the Shanti Parva of the Mahabharata*

NEW EDUCATION CAN MAKE THE WORLD NEW

UNIVERSITIES IN ANCIENT INDIA

Towards the end of the last millennium B.C. a few cities became renowned because of their teachers. Chief among them were — Varanasi, and Kanchi (in the beginning of the Christian era). Varanasi was famous for its religious teachers. Takshashila was known for its secular studies. Among the famous men connected with Takshashila was Panini, the Grammarian, Kautilya, the Brahmin minister of Chandragupta Maurya and Charaka, one of the two leading authorities of Indian medical sciences. Takshashila and Ujjain also taught Medicine, Mathematics and Astronomy. In the south, Kanchi became an important center of learning. Hiuen Tsang remarks that Vallabhi was as great as Nalanda and Vikramashila.

Although the Smritis maintained that a small number of students study under a single teacher, the university towns had thousands of students and a number of teachers. The whole establishment was maintained by charitable patrons. Ideally, the teacher asked no fee, but the students repaid his debt by their service to the teacher. (However, a Jataka story tells us how a teacher of Takshashila treated the students well who paid him money while keeping others waiting.) It is also interesting to note that in Takshashila even married people were admitted as students.

Out of all the Universities, Nalanda was the most impressive. Eight Colleges were built by different patrons. One of the colleges was said to be four storeys high, as stated by Hiuen Tsang, the Chinese traveller.

34

EDUCATION IN ANCIENT INDIA : THE GLORIOUS HERITAGE...

Here is what a research record tells us:

Every facility existed for studying various kinds of subjects in the University. There were three great libraries as per Tibetan records. Nalanda attracted students not only from different parts of India but also from Tibet and China. The standards of examination were stiff, and only those who could pass the test prescribed by the *dvarapandita* or the scholar at the gate, were admitted to this university. Also, for being admitted to the university, candidates were required to be familiar with old and new books. Nalanda was one of the earliest examples of residential cum-teaching institutions which housed thousands of monks devoted to learning, philosophy and meditation. Over 10,000 students including teachers lived and studied at the university. They came from various parts of the world apart from India, Central Asia, China and Korea.

Though Nalanda was primarily a Buddhist university, its curricula included Hindu scriptures, philosophy and medicine, as recorded by Hiuen Tsang. Logic and exegetics were pre-eminent because these students were expected to enter into dialogue with visiting doctors of all schools. This compulsion of public debate made both teachers and students become familiar with all systems of thought in accurate summary. The university also had a succession of brilliant teachers. Dharmapala was a Tamil nobleman from Kanchi in the south. Janamitra came from another country. Silabhadra, the saintly Guru of Hiuen Tsang, came from Assam and he was a converted Brahmin. Tibetan records mention a succession of learned monks from Nalanda who visited their country. It is also said that Sudhakara Simha went to China and worked there on the translation of Buddhist texts.

EDUCATION IN ANCIENT INDIA

Perhaps these great universities declined as foreigners invaded India, and Buddhism began to lose its mass following among the people.

A young student with whom I discussed the ancient universities of India, remarked that she was amazed that Indian Universities attracted so many students in those times, without the benefit of publicity, newspapers, websites, etc. And also, that students from so many far-off countries braved all the hazards of travel across seas and mountains and strange lands, to seek learning in this country!

We owe a lot to the Indians, who taught us how to count, without which no worthwhile scientific discovery could have been made.

Albert Einstein

FOR YOUR REFLECTION:

Let Us Be Proud of Our Heritage!

The writer and historian, Sudheer Birodkar, tells us in his book *India's Contribution to World Culture:*

The human spirit in Ancient India has given to the world, the values of non-violence, religious tolerance, renunciation along with many elements of knowledge in fields like production technology, mechanical engineering, ship-building, navigation, architecture, civil engineering, medical science, physics, chemistry, logic, astronomy, mathematics and so on...

Other examples of elements of material culture and civilisation that originated in ancient India and which the world owes to the genius of ancient Indian scientists and inventors include:

- the technique of algorithm used in computer science today
- the science of algebra
- the concept of zero — on which ultimately rests the binary code which has given us all software including the WWW through which you access the internet
- the technique of manufacturing crystal (sugar)cane sugar (the word sugar is derived from the Sanskrit term "Sharkara")
- the making of camphor (this word is derived from the Sanskrit root word "Karpuram" according to the Oxford Dictionary)
- the making of tin (the technical English word for tin is Cassiterite which is said to have been derived from the Sanskrit term "Kasthira")
- the making of dyes like Anline and Indigo (the word Indigo comes from the term India and the word Anline is derived from the Arabic term An Nil which is derived from the Sanskrit term Neelam, according to the Oxford dictionary)
- the Gumbaz that we see on mosques all over the world originated as the interlocking dome in the "Stupa" of the Buddhist architectural tradition of India

IN A LIGHTER VEIN:

One of the distinguished disciples trained at Swami Sivananda's *ashrama* tells us, that in the early days, he was perplexed and puzzled by the attitude of the Guru. When he tried to refer to books to find answers to his spiritual queries, the Guru would reproach him, saying, "Why don't you ask me?" When the disciples called upon the Guru repeatedly, the opposite instructions came, "Why do you not think for yourself !" …the *shishyas* learnt to take responsibility and to think for themselves. Now, the Guru said, " Who gave you the authorisation for this?"

It was only later, that the disciples realised that they were being moulded, and being trained to acquire a balance between "dependence and independence, self reliance and interdependence."

Swami Sitaramananda, who became a respected Guru himself, says this of his Master:

"When he praised you, flattered and thanked you, it was like pin pricks. Something must be wrong! He taught us through paradoxes. Many times, I found myself thinking, "Swamiji, please make up your mind, tell us once and for all what you expect from us. It is so tiring to try to figure out what is right." Life would be easier, I thought, if only there was only one way of acting or reacting, one mode of being. On the contrary, life seemed to be quite complex, a mixture between being flexible and being strong . Head, heart, hands were put to test. Head, heart and hands were expected to work together."

SADHU VASWANI'S VISION: THE MIRA...

In the Mira Institutions education given to students is associated with the blessed name of St. Mira. And, I have said, again and again, that our education should not merely be *associated* with Mira's name, but should be *rooted* in the teaching of Mira's songs and Mira's life.

Sadhu Vaswani

THE MIRA MOVEMENT IS BORN

In the 1930's, the education scenario in India was not promising. The more Sadhu Vaswani reflected on it, the more he felt that the current education system was failing to serve state and society. Imbued himself in the ideals of *rishis* of ancient India, he was deeply saddened to see the education of the 28th century moving farther and farther away from those values and ideals.

As he surveyed this situation, a deep sadness crept into his soul. Schools and colleges, he said to himself, must be freed from alien influences, and the ideals that inspired education in ancient India must be rediscovered and introduced in our institutions – if India was to make its contribution to human civilisation, and add to the freshness of human life in the future.

In conversation with his devotees, one day, he expressed his opinion that what India needed most was a new Education. This was met with great enthusiasm from earnest volunteers, who felt that the Master would indeed, be rendering a great service to the society by starting such a movement.

And so it came to pass, that, on the evening of June 3, 1933, as he paced to and fro on his terrace with a far-away, dreamy look in his mystic eyes, he heard within him, a voice urging him to initiate new lines in education.

It was a stupendous task. It would need a lot of money. He put his hand into his shirt pocket and drew out his purse. There was a two-paise* coin in it. That was all the money he had with him at the moment.

What should he do?

Again, the Voice spoke, "Give all you have – and the All-in-all will not fail you!"

In the early hours of the dawn of June 4, 1933, amidst the chanting of Vedic *mantras,* he kindled the sacred *havan* fire, and announced the opening of St. Mira's School for Girls at Hyderabad-Sind.

---

*In those days a rupee consisted of sixteen *annas* or 64 *paise*.

Solemnly, he handed over the two-paise coin to Mrs. Parpati Malkani, the Secretary of the Sakhi Satsang. "Our new school will be started with this blessed two-paise coin," he told the assembled devotees – words which have gone down in golden letters in the history of the Mira Movement in Education.

Sadhu Vaswani's Vision: The Mira Movement in Education

The torch of the Mira Education, lit by my Beloved Master in 1933, celebrated its Platinum Jubilee year in 2008. I am indeed indebted to the grace of Guru and God which has enabled the Sadhu Vaswani Mission to carry forward the educational activities that were so dear to my Master.

Today, the MIRA Institutions – among which we include no less than three Sadhu Vaswani International schools run by the Mission Centres all over India, as well as the schools and a college in Pune founded by Sadhu Vaswani himself – offer their unique brand of value-based education to over fifteen thousand students, from the pre-primary to post-graduate stage. The Sadhu Vaswani College of Nursing was inaugurated in the year 2006; and the Sadhu Vaswani Institute of Management Studies was inaugurated in July 2010, at the Mira College Campus at Koregaon Park, Pune.

What is special about St. Mira's education? Let me reply, using, as far as possible, Sadhu Vaswani's own words:

- We believe that education is a matter of the Spirit – and not just acquisition of paper degrees.

- The end of all knowledge is service– service of the poor and the lowly, the sick and the afflicted, the halt and the handicapped.

- While our students are taught and trained to show good results in their examinations, the emphasis is always on character building, service, heroic living and spiritual unfolding.

- True education cannot stop with the development of the brain alone, Sadhu Vaswani insisted. Therefore the Mira Education aims at triple training – of the head, the hand and the heart.

- Sadhu Vaswani's ideals for Mira school were indeed lofty. He wanted it to be an ideal institution – and for its teachers and students to reflect those ideals in deeds of daily living. Thus he gave Mira Institutions a four-fold ideal: Simplicity and Service, Purity and Prayer.

NEW EDUCATION CAN MAKE THE WORLD NEW

Why Mira?

Sadhu Vaswani saw St. Mira as a free spirit. She was possessed of true *bhakti* – dedication; absolute and total. In his immortal words:

> St. Mira was an advocate of that true freedom for women, which grows out of love of God and service of the poor. With one strong sweep of her soul she rose heroically to break the fetters of Indian womanhood. She called them to join her in processions where the name of God was sung. She called them to form *kirtan* groups. She asked them to build their freedom in the message of the Flute.

10 The Mira education aims at awakening consciousness to light, to joy. "Hitch your wagon to the star!" is the call of St. Mira's schools to their students. Youth is hope, not despair! And if our beloved but broken India is to be rebuilt, it needs, in different parts, youths full of hope and faith and courage to lay a spiritual foundation of a new nation.

Sadhu Vaswani

11 Vaswaniji's services to education in India have been unique... I feel that St. Mira's school is... an oasis in our educational desert...

Dr. G.S. Arundale
President, Theosophical Society

WHAT THE MIRA MOVEMENT STANDS FOR:

As Sadhu Vaswani visualised it, the Mira Institutions stood for a new type of education, with emphasis on five vital aspects:

1. **Quality in Education:** Students are taught to have faith in themselves. "Believe in yourselves," the students are taught, "believe and achieve!"

2. **Character:** Character-building education is what the Mira Institutions aim at. The emphasis is not on text books, but on the following qualities of character:

   - **Courage:** The great word of the Mira School is *shakti*. Be strong, every Mira student is urged; meet failure with success! Work on in strength of body and mind and heart, and the will-to-achieve.

   - **The value of games:** The Mira Movement believes in the moulding power of games. Physical discipline and fitness are important, for the body is, after all, a temple which houses the eternal soul – the *atman*. Sadhu Vaswani often said: "Body-building is nation-building." According to him, *pranayama* and meditation helped in building the student's power of concentration.

- Student-teacher dialogue: The word, *character*, radically means *impression*. And the one who can impress the student best, is a true teacher. Such teachers inspire trust. True education is a dialogue between the teacher and the pupil; it is a communion of their minds and hearts – one with the other.

- Discipline: the secret of true discipline is voluntary obedience, not compulsion, which only arouses rebelliousness in the students. In the Mira School, discipline is not *interference* with the pupil, but an endeavour to influence him/her for the better.

- Reverence for All Life: This includes reverence for those above us, the great heroes of humanity, the saints, sages and servants of East and West, who have left behind their legacy for the world to benefit from. Reverence for what is around us – which includes this great planet, the human community, the world we live in. Reverence too, for what is beneath us – for Sadhu Vaswani firmly believed that birds and animals are man's younger brothers and sisters, in the One family of creation. Sadhu Vaswani urged that "to build up India's destiny anew, we need to be in touch with agricultural needs, with peasants and labourers." "Cities," Sadhu Vaswani said, "are soulless." And the Mira Movement will become a real movement of new education by "opening centres of true Indian Culture in India's villages and draw together the village folk in the service of Indian ideas."

3. Community service: Education is not complete, unless knowledge and wisdom are translated into service of humanity. In emphasising community service, the students are taught to move away from self-centred, narrow living, and to think of others, especially those less fortunate than ourselves.

4. Love of Indian ideals and reverence for humanity: If we are to build India anew, we must show our students that nationalism is not narrow and parochial; we must teach them that imitation of the West is emaciation of culture. We must teach them above all, that India stands for the supremacy of the soul. True India is not what politicians build: for what they build today will go down tomorrow. There is an India that is eternal: it is the India of the sages, the *rishis*, the India of Sri Rama and Sri Krishna, the Buddha and Mahavira, St. Mira and Guru Nanak, the India of Sri Chaitanya and Sant Kabir. Of this India, St. Mira's students are taught, again and again,

and urged to dedicate themselves to the service of the motherland and the great cause of World Peace.

5. **Global vision:** The students are taught to see that their nationalism and patriotism are not reduced to narrow egoism. St. Mira's students are imbued with the concept of Universal brotherhood and Peace. It was Sadhu Vaswani's vision that every teacher and every student of the Mira Institution should be an ambassador of humanity.

"Cultivate the soul!" was Sadhu Vaswani's message to the Mira Institutions. He felt this was the urgent need of India and its youth, its community and its public life. This, he felt, was the secret at the heart of St. Mira's songs. This, too, was the message of India's ancient *rishis* to the world – "Cultivate The Soul!"

How do the Mira Institutions translate these ideals into the reality of their academic life?

Each and every Mira teacher, each and every Mira student will tell you, it is not easy, in these troubled times we live in! But each one of them also believes that the grace and benign blessings of their Rev. Founder are always guiding them, guarding them and inspiring them to live up to those ideals, in the best way they are capable of!

To this end, all Mira Institutions have adapted certain modalities of functioning, certain unique practices.

The first among these is the daily Sanctuary period – a period of 'retreat', a period reserved for reflection, prayer and silence, attended by the entire school/college.

This concept is so vital to the Mira Institutions, that visitors to our colleges and schools are invariably amazed and profoundly impressed by the atmosphere, the collective vibrations and the aura they find in these gatherings.

Sadhu Vaswani did not merely specify the Sanctuary as a 'compulsory' period; he also gave it a theme – "The Art of Living" – and this was as early as in 1933.

The students are taught the great truth that they are not the bodies they wear. Each one of them is essentially an immortal soul.

---

12 I have great respect for the saintly character and life of Shri. T. L. Vaswani ... I have been, for many years, following the activities of his Mira Movement in Education with great joy ... Those who are inspired by his ideals of saintliness, devotion to duty and dedication to service, will be good citizens of our country ...

Dr. Sarvapalli Radhakrishnan
Former President of India

> **SADHU VASWANI ON THE SANCTUARY:**
>
> The Mira School, through its Sanctuary Period – the opening period in the school's programme – draws the attention of the pupils to the wisdom of the *rishis* and the sages of humanity. Love for the motherland is taught as an essential element in character building – but we also teach that the truly great ones are not a monopoly of India, but have appeared in all countries, and have enriched the lives of all races, and inspired and illumined all religions. We teach our students, therefore, to respect all races and religions.

The Mira Institutions emphasise the principle of *ahimsa* – non-violence and therefore urge their students to refrain from food of violence. They also teach the students to approach every animal, every bird, every creature in a spirit of reverence – for birds and beasts too, are, like us, God's children.

St. Mira's Movement, as we have emphasised, aims at "an integral education", as Sadhu Vaswani described it. Thus, the Mira Institutions provide an academic environment where humanism is blended with the spiritual ideal. Sadhu Vaswani believed that the *secular*, in its right expression, is *humanistic:* the truly secular, he insisted, cannot be cut off from what is really the root of all existence – the Spirit.

Thus, to St. Mira's students is passed on the teaching that to love God and love their country, are not abstract ideals – but a rich reality, which expresses itself in and through the spirit of service and sacrifice.

The days sacred to the great ones of humanity, the sages who have appeared alike in East and West, are solemnly observed in the Mira Institutions. Sri Krishna and Sri Rama, Gautama Buddha and Jesus, Guru Nanak and Sant Kabir, Prophet Muhammad and St. Mira, Sri Ramakrishna and St. Francis, Father Damien and Mother Teresa, Mahavir and Mahatma Gandhi, Lokamanya Tilak and Vivekananda and others like them, are remembered and honoured on days sacred to their memories.

While the Mira schools emphasise the teachings of the Gita – the Scripture of Light, the Bible of Humanity – they also believe that in *all* scriptures of *all* races and religions, the one Light shines! So the Mira students listen to readings from the sacred texts of Hindus and Muslims,

NEW EDUCATION CAN MAKE THE WORLD NEW

Sikhs and Christians, Buddhists and Jains.

The Mira students are taught to respect work and labour. Thus there is emphasis on crafts, on practical applications and skills. Students are also taught to recognise the spiritual character of everyday work — work directed by the spirit of justice and truth. For such work is truly worship of God.

Service of the poor and needy, of the sick and suffering ones, service of the criminals and the deprived and downtrodden, are an integral part of the Mira education.

Community welfare is built into the academic structure, so that each and every class undertakes a meaningful social service activity — visiting institutions for the visually handicapped, homes for the aged, orphanages, hospitals, slums, construction sites and outlying villages; as well as inviting inmates from such institutions to attend special programmes at the school or college. *Bal-melas* or fun-fairs are organised for underprivileged children. N.S.S. students visit villages to offer *shram dhan*. Even today, some students get together with their teachers, and cook food with their own hands, to serve these brothers and sisters.

Mira students are necessarily trained to show good results in the examinations; but they are also taught that life is larger than livelihood, that the end of education is not just gains in silver and gold, but the cultivation of the soul. The cult of the ego, they are taught, can never lead to true happiness. Rather, true happiness begins only when they get out of their little selves, leaving their ego behind,

---

13 Holy, holy, holy is every creature! Touch ye these children of the Lord with reverence and love! Harm them not! But serve them in deep humility! These birds and beasts, these animals, these creatures, children of Krishna, are the forms the Lord hath put on!

Sadhu Vaswani

---

14 Gather knowledge for service: gather knowledge and be ready for that true life which is one of offering — the life of *yagna* — and see that you do nothing to dishonour your noble heritage, the noblest one can have in any part of the world, the heritage of India's *rishis* and seers, the heritage of St. Mira!

Sadhu Vaswani
Addressing St. Mira's students

and turn towards the ideals of service and sacrifice.

True education, Sadhu Vaswani believed, is a Science of Life. And therefore, true educators cannot merely be teachers, lecturers or professors: the ideal Mira teacher is encouraged to be a friend and guide on the path of life.

Before each Mira teacher is placed Sadhu Vaswani's ideal: "The teacher is a friend! A friend of brother teachers, a friend of all pupils, a friend of all races and communities, a friend of all nations, of all men and birds and beasts, a friend of God's creation!"

> **15** Friendship is the essence of true education. The teacher is a true friend of his pupils — friend and guide, and therefore, the true director. This significant thought is uttered by Plato in one of his *Dialogues,* when he says that the secret of education is friendship. Is not the same thought expressed in the Gita too, in the words: *Shraddavaan labhate gnanam?...* Shraddha is reverence, which includes humility and friendship.
>
> *Sadhu Vaswani*

IN A LIGHTER VEIN . . .

I am often asked by my younger friends, whether it is possible to inculcate the Mira ideals and values – Simplicity and Service, Purity and Prayer, among the older students of the colleges. Many of them regard even our daily Sanctuary, as an "unnecessary discipline".

I am aware that many of our senior students 'cut out' the sanctuary almost on a daily basis – but we have no plans to drop the required attendance from the college schedule. I personally believe that the daily joint prayer-cum-reflection meeting is the glue that holds the Mira Institution together.

I must also add, that when I travel from place to place, I often meet former Mira students, who freely confess to me that their education at St. Mira's was indeed a glorious period in their lives.

Many of them also tell me, with a little embarrassment, that while they did everything they could to "bunk" the daily sanctuary period, they realised later that the Sanctuary taught them far more than the rest of their education!

J. P. Vaswani

WHAT AILS EDUCATION TODAY?

The education that is being given in our schools and colleges today, emphasises merely book-learning. Students are asked to study a few books, 'cram' certain facts, memorise them and reproduce them. We 'pump' dry facts and figures into their unresponsive heads, for we have forgotten the true meaning of the word 'education'.

'Education' according to its Latin origins, means 'drawing out'. That is what education is – a *drawing out* process. Alas, we have turned it upside down, into a pumping-in process!

J. P. Vaswani

WHAT AILS EDUCATION TODAY?

What Science has not Taught Us...

Maxim Gorky, the great Russian thinker and writer, was one day addressing a huge rally of peasants in Russia. He spoke to them about the benefits of science. Raising his voice to make his point, he proclaimed loudly, "Consider what benefits science had brought to you! Science has taught you how to fly in the air like a bird, and science has taught you how to dive into the depths of the ocean like a fish. Is this not marvellous?"

A poor, illiterate peasant got up and said to Gorky, "True it is, that science has taught us how to fly in the air like a bird, and swim in the depths of the ocean, like a fish. But, alas, science has not taught us how to live on earth in love and peace and amity, like good human beings!"

What Ails Education Today?

Modern education has sharpened the brain – but in the process, it seems to have hardened the heart!

The bitter truth is that current education has failed in its most crucial task – the task of cultivating character. It has emphasised the development of the brain. Brain power is so well developed that we now create what is called 'artificial intelligence'. Technological progress has been tremendous; science has marched on rapidly; but the problems we face today, will not be solved by brain power alone!

Consider what some 'educated' people are up to, these days:

- Fresh graduates want jobs that pay them fat salaries. Naturally! But the other side of the coin is that those who join the 'rat race' for higher paychecks and better designations are unable to quit: in other words, having joined the rat race, they stay rats all their working lives.

- Ethics and values, principles and morals are thrown to the winds, in the search for more money and more comforts. Educated people break the laws ruthlessly in this country: they ignore traffic rules; they cheat on taxes; they bribe their way to government sanctions. They do not hesitate to defraud others, if it is to their own advantage.

- The teaching profession is in a near state of crisis. Our best students refuse to consider teaching even as a remote option. Those who do aspire to become teachers cannot clear the State Level/National Eligibility tests! (SLET/NET). In fact, I am reliably informed that the national average for NET and SLET is about 3 – 4%. Out of every hundred post graduates who opt for teaching, only four actually reach the required level of eligibility!

- The bulk of our graduates seek easy money, by means of jobs that do not tax their brains: thus tens of thousands of youngsters are queuing up outside call centres, retail chains, airlines and TV studios. Science, Mathematics, Philosophy and Physics departments in colleges are facing closure. Senior academicians and thinkers are worried: how can we survive without pure sciences and basic research? How can we remain civilised if we neglect philosophy and the liberal arts?

- Students who have obtained degrees in Engineering and Medicine are turning to Management Diplomas in their 30's:

WHAT AILS EDUCATION TODAY?

the reason is that they want more money. Young men and women who have cleared the Civil Service examinations and joined the public administration are quitting their jobs for lucrative private sector service. This is obviously leading to a lopsided growth.

- Cyber crime – fakes – frauds – forgeries – scams – scandals: these are some of the 'sophisticated' misdemeanors of 'educated' people.

- Systematic and deliberate destruction of the environment: the illiterate poor of the world have neither the means nor the methods to accomplish this. After all it was 'superior technology' that gave us CFC, spray cans, non-biodegradable plastics and other such things which successfully managed to tear a gaping hole in the ozone layer! Not to forget 'entrepreneurs' who are cutting down forests to build five-star hotels, and endangering finely balanced eco-systems in the name of 'progress' and 'development'.

- The 'obsessive' focus on individual achievement and brilliance is also leading our youngsters astray; we fail to emphasise team-spirit, community welfare and overall development.

- The contemporary, much-talked about goals of 'empowerment' and 'achievement' seem to be reserved only for the intellectual elite, who want nothing to do with the underprivileged, downtrodden classes.

- Conversely, the emphasis of the government on numbers and quantity is playing havoc with the quality of higher education.

- Recently, the Government of India set up a Knowledge Commission to look into issues and problems of higher education in the country. However, many of the recommendations made by the commission have not been accepted, (leave alone implemented) by the government.

- Indian education continues to neglect India's rich heritage: Kautilya's *Arthashastra* is studied by foreigners; the concept of Ram Rajya (selfless, fair and just governance dedicated to the welfare of the people) is dismissed as a 'Hindu' and therefore, unacceptable ideal. Ayurveda, Siddha and Yunani medicine do not get the attention they richly deserve.

> **16** The state shall endeavour to provide within a period of ten years from the commencement of this Constitution, for free and compulsory education for all children until they complete the age of fourteen years.
>
> *Article 45 of the Indian Constitution*

NEW EDUCATION CAN MAKE THE WORLD NEW

DID YOU KNOW . . . ?

- Some years ago, an eminent thinker and educationist, Sri M. N. Roy, set up the *Indian Renaissance Institute* at Dehradun. His aim was to bring scholars and researchers together to revive and imbibe the best and most positive aspects of Indian heritage so as to bring about a rebirth of Indian culture and tradition. Unfortunately, he died before his worthy aim could be accomplished.

- A few years ago, every educated Indian celebrated it as a personal triumph, when Dr. Amartya Sen, the Indian born economist, was awarded the Nobel Prize. We honoured him too, with the Bharat Ratna – the nation's highest civilian award. But Dr. Sen's fundamental thesis – that without universal education, real development is not possible – has not been taken seriously by any of us!

- Universal education, eradicating illiteracy, is actually being placed in conflict with the so called anti-poverty programmes of the government. In fact, there are politicians and social activists who argue that Poverty eradication must take precedence over universal primary education – the classic chicken-or-egg-first syndrome!

- It is widely agreed that lack of education is the basic cause of many social evils like female infanticide, caste discrimination and child labour which still persist in our society.

FACT FILE

The Tata Institute of Social Sciences, Mumbai, estimates that one in every three young people, is still illiterate – 60 years after independence.

17

Basic education, good health, and other human attainments are not only directly valuable as constituent elements of our basic capabilities, these capabilities can also help in generating economic success of a more standard kind, which in turn can contribute to the quality of life even more... The remarkable neglect of elementary education in India is all the more striking given the widespread recognition, in the contemporary world, of the importance of basic education for economic development. Somehow the educational aspects of economic development have continued to be out of the main focus.

Amartya Sen

WHAT AILS EDUCATION TODAY?

Reviewing a book on *Fifty Years Of Higher Education in India,* C. T. Kurien writes:

> "Problems relating to higher education – privatisation and commercialisation, political interference and corruption, mismanagement and agitations, falling standards and irrelevance – are topics of public discussion almost on a day-to-day basis."

Thus far, I have only spoken of the little that I have seen, felt and heard from friends about the problems that beset Indian education *in general.*

To talk about the problem of special education – education of the rural poor, women's education, restructuring professional /vocational education, education for the handicapped and the mentally challenged . . . a whole book could be written on each of these aspects!

My aim is not to denigrate the system, nor to devalue the considerable achievements we have made. Rather, my dearest wish is that India, which is today being described as the Super Power of the future, must also make its unique and rich contribution to the world's culture and civilisation, as a force to reckon within the educational sphere!

Today, in India, as in the world, chaotic forces are gathering strength. The forces of darkness seem to choke the voice of light. Today, both knowledge and power are being perverted into instruments of social chaos and destruction. Today, the moral base of public life seems to have shattered. Today, intellectual honesty and self-discipline are conspicuous by their absence. Today, our administration is being destroyed by the malignant cancer of corruption ... Therefore, today, more than ever before, we need a new type of education which will emphasise the spiritual and moral values of life.

For your Reflection

- Does our education encourage students to develop the spirit of courage?
- Do we teach our youngsters to respect truth and stand up for truth even though the heaven's fall?
- Do we inculcate in them the value of purity in their personal lives?
- Do we emphasise the need for selfless service to society?

If you find yourself answering 'No' to more than one of the above questions, you must conclude that our education has failed us! That we need a new education which may offer the students an integral training of the head, the hand and heart; and a proper discipline of willpower and the emotions.

> **18** The end of all education, all training, should be man-making. The end and aim of all training is to make the man grow. The training by which the current and expression of the will are brought under control and become fruitful is called education.
>
> *Swami Vivekananda*

IN A LIGHTER VEIN

An American explorer travelled to a remote corner of the world, where no white man had ever set foot. In the dark depths of the forests, he came across a party of cannibals who were presiding over the killing and 'roasting' of a human victim. To his horror of horrors, he recognised the chief of the cannibals – it was a man who had been his batch-mate at an American University of repute!

Shocked and pained by this discovery, he appealed to his erstwhile friend, "You have been educated at one of the world's best universities. How – oh, *how* could you continue this barbaric practice of eating human flesh?"

The cannibal chief replied, without batting an eyelid, "Of course my education has made a difference to me. I now eat human flesh with a knife and fork!"

WOMEN'S EDUCATION

The woman-soul has the *shakti* to rebuild the shattered world in the strength of her intuitions, her purity, her simplicity, her spiritual aspirations, her sympathy and silent sacrifice. The woman-soul will lead us upward, on!

Sadhu Vaswani

Maitreyi's Aspiration

Maitreyi was one of the most distinguished and pre-eminently wise women of ancient India. Athirst with keen aspiration to gain knowledge of the Vedas and Upanishads and the sacred *Shastras*, she became the wife of sage Yagnavalkya.

Although she performed her duties as a *rishi patni* with meticulous care and devotion, Maitreyi was constantly in quest of the supreme knowledge that would transcend the material life of this world. Above all, therefore, she longed to be a *shishya,* a true disciple to her husband.

Rishi Yagnavalkya, who was then engaged in compiling and codifying his *Yagnavalkya Smriti (*on Jurisprudence and Law), decided to seek *sanyasa*. He explained his decision to his two wives, Khatyayani and Maitreyi, and assured them that adequate provision would be made for their comfortable life even after he left his *ashrama.*

Khatyayani, a simple, obedient and devout woman, accepted her husband's instructions without protest. But Maitreyi could not be put off so easily.

"Dear husband, I pray you, tell me one thing before you leave," she begged the Rishi. "You have very kindly said that you are leaving for me an adequate settlement to support myself in your absence. Is the wealth enough to assure me of immortality?"

The Rishi smiled. "You will be wealthy in worldly riches," he said. "But you know, my dear, that wealth cannot make you immortal."

"Should you leave me the wealth of all this world," Maitreyi continued, "would I become immortal thereby?"

"No, no, Maitreyi," the Rishi said to her patiently. "No one ever attained immortality on account of their wealth."

"In that case," said Maitreyi humbly, "of what use is the settlement which cannot lead me to the goal I seek? Therefore, tell me how I may attain what I seek."

Yagnavalkya was so pleased with this earnest request. In his unsurpassed spiritual wisdom, he realised her earnest aspiration, and revealed to her the supreme knowledge of the *Atman.*

The immortal dialogue between Yagnavalkya and Maitreyi is recorded in the *Brihadaranyaka Upanishad.*

Women's Education

"Education," said the philosopher, Will Durant, "is the transmission of civilisation."

Truer words were never spoken! And, if education were indeed the transmission of civilisation, who is it that deserves to be educated, but woman, the transmitter of tradition and culture from one generation to another!

Woman is the architect of the new generation. Woman is the builder of the home – the first centre where children's character is built. (School comes later.) When the child's mind is still plastic, the mother influences it to grow in the right direction.

Rightly has it been said, that if you educate a man, you educate an individual; education contributes to his individual growth; it becomes his 'private property', as it were. But when you educate a woman, you educate the entire family!

Therefore, did Sadhu Vaswani describe the woman as the symbol of *Shakti*. This *shakti* is not a physical force, but the power of integration. And to the development of *stree shakti*, he devoted his vision of the Mira Movement in Education.

Why was the Mira Movement specially focussed on women, many people have asked me. The answers are straightforward, as Sadhu Vaswani gave them!

- Current education only separates and divides; a new education of integration is what we need, to stop the disintegration of our culture and civilisation. Woman is the centre of social integration. Therefore, Mira Education focuses on women.

- The values the world needs most today are simplicity, service, prayer, purity and sacrifice. It is the woman, through her intuitive affinity to these values, who can transmit them for the new generation to imbibe.

- The man-made civilisation is today broken and bleeding. We can see that man has had his chance but masculine mentality has blundered. Now, woman must get her chance, for it is she who is called upon to build a new world.

- India and the world today, need the help and inspiration of the woman-soul. It is all the more necessary to educate girls in the right atmosphere of spiritual sympathy.

WOMEN'S EDUCATION IN INDIA

Ancient India always insisted on the spiritual equality of man and woman. In the Vedic period, woman had access to the kind of education they sought. But down the ages, they lost this privilege.

In the British period, there was a revival of interest in women's education. Eminent Indians like Raja Ram Mohan Roy, Ishwar Chandra Vidya Sagar, Jyotibha Phule and his wife Savitribai Phule and E.V.R. Periyar, took laudable efforts to give women access to education.

An educated woman, who becomes a wife and mother, contributes greatly to social development:

- She makes the home a centre of light, peace and harmony.
- She improves the quality of life at home, and also outside the home.
- She imparts values and knowledge to her children, in their early, impressionable years.
- She provides guidance and support to her children when they need it most.
- She ensures that her daughters are educated.
- An alert, aware, sensitive, educated mother is undoubtedly the best teacher any child can have.

NEW EDUCATION CAN MAKE THE WORLD NEW

How can we call a nation truly civilised, if half its population is uneducated?

Many scholars and thinkers agree that lack of education has been the major obstacle on the path of women's attainment of equality with men. Only a hundred years ago, women were confined to the home, and treated like second-class citizens, and denied access to higher education. Even upper class families thought it sufficient to see to their daughters' 'accomplishments' like singing, dancing, music, painting, rather than offer them 'education' as we understand it.

Thus, women played no role in politics and governance; women could not vote; women could not enter professions; women could not inherit property.

How did they manage to break free from these severe constraints? Only through the power of education!

Education is the key to the empowerment of women today. It gives them

- Self-worth
- Self-respect
- The power of choice
- Decision making abilities
- The power to change themselves and society

Orthodox men often feared that an educated woman would cease to fulfil her traditional roles as wife and mother, if she received higher education! In America, people actually felt that a woman risked brain-fever and sterility, if she taxed herself with academic pursuits!

LET US REFLECT...

While some of us talk of empowering women and promoting the rights of the girl-child, the harsh reality is that millions and millions of girls in India are denied access to education.

What do they do instead?

- They are sent to graze cattle / collect fuel/ fetch water in villages.
- They are sent off to work as domestic labour.
- They are 'married off' and forced to bear the burden of families before they attain emotional maturity.

Thus, much needs to be done in the area of women's education.

Do women need special education?

I strongly believe they do.

Many of you may not agree with this view – but women always have, and always will occupy a special place in the home, in society, in human relationships and in moulding the generations of the future.

As such, they do require a special education, in a special environment, with special values.

Please do not take this to mean that I wish to relegate women's education to 'domestic' science, home economics, food, nutrition, etc.

Some of the best doctors, administrators, organisers, philanthropists, computer specialists, mathematicians, scientists and thinkers I have come across are women of whom I am proud!

In that case, why do I insist that women require special education and special training?

As a mother, as a wife, as a binding force in the family and society, as a transmitter of values, as an upholder of culture and tradition, the woman is called upon to play multiple roles and functions in every stage, every age, of human civilisation. It is in this recognition of her onerous responsibilities that Indian tradition accords a special value to the woman.

The woman is a valuable link between the past, present and future. Quoting one of her conversations with her guru and mentor, Swami Vivekananda, Sister Nivedita writes:

He (Swami Vivekananda) could not foresee a Hindu woman of the future entirely without the old power of meditation. Modern science woman must learn; but not at the cost of ancient spirituality... He saw clearly enough that the ideal education... would be that which would best enable every woman in time to

> **FACT FILE**
>
> In four major Indian states - Bihar, UP, Rajasthan and Delhi- over 50% girls drop out of schools between Class V and Class VI.
>
> The reasons given are the same: they have to look after siblings; they have to attend to domestic chores; or they have to work to support the family.

NEW EDUCATION CAN MAKE THE WORLD NEW

Sister Nivedita

come, to receive into herself the spiritual shakti and vitality of all the great Indian women of the past."

The land of Sita, the land of Gargi and Maitreyi, the home of Andal and Mira must accord a special place for women to facilitate their spiritual and intellectual growth!

Purity, prayer, simplicity, service, sacrifice, spirituality – are not these innate qualities of the ideal Indian woman? Is she not at once a picture of peace, harmony, prosperity, courage and wisdom? Is she not Lakshmi, Durga and Saraswati in one manifestation? Has it not been her privilege to attain the heights of love and compassion, devotion and piety, commitment and dedication to duty?

Our education must continue to stress upon these ideals, and make young women sensitive to them. Their modern aspirations will continue to be supported and sustained by these ideals.

IN A LIGHTER VEIN...

Q: Why aren't women as successful, or even more successful than men?

A: Because they have only their husbands – who can never give them the support and the sensible advice they need to be successful!

EDUCATION: THE UNFULFILLED NEED

If there is one thing that India needs today, it is men and women of character; men and women of sterling qualities, men and women whom the lust of office will not lead astray, men and women whom the gains of office will not betray; men and women who will not scramble for office or power but will use all their power in a spirit of humility in the service of India's teeming millions.

The question is: What are we doing to instil these qualities in our students?

J. P. Vaswani

EDUCATION: THE UNFULFILLED NEED

The Wisest Man

One day, as Socrates was walking with his devoted disciples, a group of young men approached him and greeted him with the words: "We hail you, O Socrates, as the wisest man in all Greece!"

Socrates laughed outright and asked them, "Who says so?"

"The Oracle has spoken," they said, "The voice has spoken, and the voice has said that Socrates is the wisest man in all Greece."

"How can I be the wisest man in Greece?" Socrates protested. "How can that be so?"

After a moment's reflection, he added, "Yes, perhaps it is true. For I am the only man in Greece who knows that he knows nothing."

Education: The Unfulfilled Need

I have said this earlier, and I say it to you again: all over the world today, schools and colleges and universities are multiplying. In India, we are getting more IITs, IIMs, more Central Universities, more Deemed Universities and more Institutes of Research.

The students in all these Institutions will be taught more subjects than their grandparents could ever dream of! There are colleges that teach Catering, Tourism and Travel, Aviation, Hospitality, Gemmology and Event Management. There are prestigious institutes to teach Fashion Designing, Photography, Film-making and Floriculture. Our students are taught so many subjects – but they are not taught the *one* subject that they need to learn above all else: how to live in the right way!

What do I mean by living in the right way?

It is my humble conviction that our students and indeed, all of us, need to be taught the following:

- how to develop our will-power
- how to control our temper
- how to use our imagination in such a way as to make our life positive and worthwhile
- how to curb our selfish impulses and grow in the spirit of sacrifice
- how to grow in the spirit of altruism
- how to be honest and cultivate the attitude of fair-play with everyone
- how to make friends – and keep them
- how to focus our energies and utilise the same for the service of suffering humanity
- how to grow in the spirit of courage, compassion and reverence for all life
- how to pray and rely on God for all our needs
- how to express the *Atman* in all the activities of daily life
- how to grow in perfection, from more to more!

Our social scientists and psychologists are concerned with the growing crime rates in society. Why do people turn to crime? Why is it that good men sometimes turn into criminals? A man commits a crime only because he does not know how to live in the right way! We send these criminals to prison, where they only slide further down the deep pit of degradation. Would it not be far better if, as children, they are sent to schools which will *prevent* them from turning to a life of crime?

Alas, in the current system, our students are only taught to read certain books, write certain set answers and work out a few prescribed 'sums' or mathematical problems. They are taught to remember certain facts and figures which are pumped into their heads. The ultimate test we set before them is to reproduce these facts and figures in the examination hall. The moment they leave the examination hall, they forget everything they have studied!

One of my friends, an experienced Professor, serves as the Placement officer in the institution where he teaches. He once said to me that HR managers from companies who come to them for campus recruitment, often tell him that whatever the students have 'studied' or 'learnt' during their graduation is irrelevant and immaterial to the company. "We have to make them *unlearn* many things that are taught here, and *relearn* what we want from our business perspective," one of them said to my friend. "The truth is, the degree you bestow on them is just a paper qualification."

Recruiters have a different agenda from the one I have been talking about; they feel that the 'paper qualification' that the student acquires really does not help him to face the world of work. What they feel is that the brighter students obtain considerable 'subject knowledge', which weaker students do not grasp; but both groups fail to acquire what are known as 'life skills' such as:

- communication skills – the ability to use language effectively, to speak, listen and write well
- people skills – the ability to interact with customers, colleagues and the general public
- soft skills – the ability to persuade, convince, socialise and make a good impression on the people they meet

Companies feel that we are not educating the students to fit into the work profiles they need; society lacks the contribution that can be made only by the truly cultured and educated youth. What then is the function of our education system?

EDUCATION: THE UNFULFILLED NEED

Train the Heart!

What we need then, is a system of education that will awaken the *hearts* of our students! It is the heart that needs to be trained, for noble feelings and impulses that arise in the heart, must guide the intellect towards right actions: the heart is the master, the brain is but the servant. Of what use is an education that trains the servant, but neglects the master?

Let me illustrate this in terms of those 'life skills' we mentioned earlier. Imagine a senior executive, who needs to take a quick, tough decision: his emotions must be under firm control so that his intellect can function efficiently to analyse, understand and solve the problem. Or, to take a different situation, let us consider the bureaucrat who is being offered a hefty bribe to 'pass' a certain file; his intellect is sufficiently alert to know that he is doing something that is morally reprehensible; but the feeling of greed gets the better of him, and he succumbs to corruption.

That is why, I repeat, our students must be taught to live a life that is clean, honest and incorruptible; they need to be taught the courage to stand up for what is right, and to heed the still, clear voice of their conscience at all times!

What is Missing?

Our students have not been taught that life and all the bounties of life are given to us as a *trust* – I repeat, a *trust* – to be spent in the service of those less fortunate than ourselves!

We have an elaborate infrastructure, we have a complex machinery of higher education – but I wish someone would tell me where I can find the soul, the true spirit of education.

Current education has cut itself off from great ideals, from the great soul of nature, and from the great ones of humanity. That is why so many of our 'rising stars' succumb to temptations of power and wealth.

Today in India, forces of darkness seem to choke the voices of Light. Today, both knowledge and power are being perverted into instruments of social chaos and destruction. Today, the moral base of life seems to have been shattered.

A friend said to me the other day, that there are more than three hundred websites on the internet, which can teach you how to put a bomb together! Not only are these websites accessible to everyone – the materials required to assemble a bomb can also be easily procured from the 'right' dealers in the 'grey' market.

Just consider the use to which we are putting advanced science and technology!

> Recently in Pune, raids were conducted on several diagnostic centres and clinics offering Ultrasound examinations. Can you guess the reason? They were offering their 'advanced' facilities to indicate the sex of the foetus in a pregnant woman's womb – and also offering 'facilities' to abort female foetuses – so that more and more happy parents could give birth to sons and thus dream of fat dowries to be added to the family coffers.
>
> An American scientist whom I met, told me very politely but bitterly, that no matter how hard the West strove to improve the quality of medical care, there were people in certain parts of the world who would abuse and pervert the best inventions to make more money. I was forced to hang my head down in shame!

In the last decade alone, several newly built road bridges have collapsed, causing the deaths of innocent people, apart from extensive damage to property. Reason? Use of poor quality material, shoddy construction, scant respect for safety norms on the part of civil engineers and contractors.

These are 'highly educated' people by any standard. If such is their attitude to public safety and people's lives, what can we say about the education they have received?

Little wonder then, that Sadhu Vaswani referred to the current system of education in his day as 'mis-education'.

Mis-education, he felt, only glorifies the ego; and egoism is cruelty as well as cowardice – for it ignores the claims and rights of others. Mis-education, he concluded, infects the *heart* – which is the seat of love.

"Is it not true that the hearts of many of the educated people are infected, dried?" he asked. "Passion takes the place of true affection or love in the lives of such people."

Thus, much of current education, then as now, only contributes to the disintegration of the true personality of man. Step by step does the

EDUCATION: THE UNFULFILLED NEED

disintegration deepen, until man's spirit – the *atman* – is reduced to a state in which it cannot influence the life of the individual. Man enters total darkness. In such a state, man does not know where his life is leading him, for he begins to feel that his life has no aim, no purpose. Thus an incurable pessimism sets in. This condition, the Gita refers to as *buddhi vinashanam* – the destruction of true consciousness. It is the final stage of disintegration.

True education must lift our youths out of these depths; it must awaken their consciousness to Light and Joy which is their birthright.

What India needs most today – indeed, what the world needs most today – are young men and women, enlightened, enriched with the spirit of new education.

Sadhu Hiranand, Sadhu Vaswani's inspired teacher, would often say to his students: "The heart of the world is awakening: the heart must be inspired."

Alas, men's hearts are not yet awakened – that is why we have crime, violence, terrorism, aggression and strife. The heart is not yet awakened – that is why we have fierce and selfish scrambles for power. The heart is not awakened – that is why poverty, malnutrition and early blindness afflict our rural poor, who are still ill-clothed, ill-housed and ill-fed. The heart of humanity has not yet awakened – that is why our nations are spending billions on nuclear devices, long-range missiles and weapons of mass destruction.

Education of the true type must contribute to the health and happiness of the individual – and of humanity as a whole.

---

19 From the point of view of reverence due, a teacher is three fold superior to a mere lecturer, a farmer hundred fold superior to a teacher and a woman a thousand fold superior to a farmer.

Manu Smriti

"What is the malady of modern education?" we asked Sadhu Vaswani.

He answered: **"Dissociation"**—

* **Dissociation of the heart and mind** — allowing selfishness to take hold of our lives.

* **Dissociation of the heart and the senses** — so that the senses fail to listen to the still, small voice of the heart and do not become purified.

EDUCATION AS COMMERCE

The University Grants Commission, the Central Government and the State Governments are making relentless efforts to curb the malpractice of 'capitation fees' and 'donations' charged by institutions to grant admission for Professional courses. But what remains a mystery is why middle class parents are willing to sell their land, mortgage their houses and pawn their jewels to pay over Fifty Lakh rupees or even more, for a Medical seat!

A social worker had the chance to interact with the parents of a student, who were desperate to procure a Medical seat for their son, at whatever cost.

"Fifty lakhs is a lot of money," she tried to reason with them. "How can you justify that kind of money on a degree?"

"It is not an expense, it is only an investment," was the mother's reply.

"I don't understand," protested the social worker. "Your son will take five to six years to become a fully qualified doctor. And then he will have to start his career in private practice, or join a good hospital. It will be years before he earns a good salary. What kind of an investment are you talking about?"

"Madam, we are not banking on his medical practice," the father explained to her patiently. "See, we have paid only fifty lakhs as capitation fees for his Medical college seat. When he gets his degree, he can fetch one crore from the marriage market in our community! *You* tell me now – is this not a good investment?"

In A Lighter Vein . . .

Roopesh had just completed his M.Sc. examination and was mightily pleased with himself. "I'm a postgraduate in Zoology," he would say, again and again. He was certain that he would be hired very soon for a lucrative job. But he was annoyed and frustrated when his parents insisted that he should go to the village to visit his grand parents.

"What can a highly educated person like me do with those ignorant, illiterate villagers?" he complained loudly. "You seem to forget I am a post graduate in Zoology ."

On the day he arrived in the village, his grandparents heard that sentence at least a dozen times.

At lunchtime, he happened to glance at the backyard, and was surprised to see an ox, patiently pulling the yoke attached to an old-fashioned oil press. His grandfather explained that as the ox went round and round, the mustard seeds in the oil press would be crushed and mustard oil extracted from them.

"But there's no one to keep an eye on the ox," said Roopesh. "How can you be sure that the job is done properly?"

His grandfather smiled and pointed to the bell tied around the neck of the ox. "That bell keeps ringing rhythmically all day," he said. "Even your grandmother, while working in the kitchen, can hear it, and she knows that the oil press is working."

Roopesh ate his lunch thoughtfully. But he pounced on his 'illiterate' grandfather with a clever question soon. "See, *Nana* – suppose the lazy ox were to stand still in one place and shake its head this way and that way, the bell would keep ringing, and all of you would be fooled, won't you?"

"He wouldn't do that," said the grandfather solemnly.

"Why not?"

"He is just an ignorant village ox," replied the old man. "He doesn't hold a postgraduate degree from any University."

A PLEA FOR VALUE-BASED EDUCATION

India's civilisation has its origin in the teachings of her great ones; and when our youths assimilate this teaching and express it in their activities and their daily life, India will step on to a new culture… a new civilisation of *shakti* in which is the hope of a new re-integrated, rejuvenated humanity.

Sadhu Vaswani

A PLEA FOR VALUE-BASED EDUCATION

HE DWELLS IN ALL

This is a precious personal memory that I am sharing with you. In my younger days, I loved to accompany Sadhu Vaswani on his evening walks. On one such walk, I saw a large, sharp-edged stone obstructing his path. Eager to be of service to the Master, I hastily stepped forward and kicked the stone aside, lest it should hurt his feet.

The moment I turned back, I knew I had done something wrong. For, there was a look of pain in Sadhu Vaswani's eyes.

"What is it, Dada?" I asked him humbly. "Have I said or done something which I should not have done? If so, pray forgive me."

In answer to my question, Sadhu Vaswani posed another question, which is etched in my mind and heart to this day. With characteristic insight, he said to me:

If God dwells in the scripture,
Does He not dwell in the stone?

I imbibed the great value of Reverence for all things, animate and inanimate, from the Master that day. I resolved then, that I would treat *everything, everyone*, with respect, love and reverence.

A Plea for Value-Based Education

At a time when darkness brooded over Western civilisation, India was strong and vital. She was acclaimed as a leader of the nations, a builder of civilisations.

Much has India suffered through the centuries. Great has been her agony. Today, she is broken, bleeding, much weakened. But India is not defeated! And she will *never* be defeated, as long as her people are aware that the Root of life is God. Turning away from God, we only wander from distraction to distraction. Therefore, this must be the first step in any value-based system of education: Turn back to God! Love God and love your fellow-men!

Therefore, let us bring God back into our schools and colleges. The state, in our country, has in several ways, repressed *dharma* in our system of education. How true are the words of the American philosopher: "If you throw God out of your schools and colleges, the vaccum thus created, will immediately be filled in by the Devil!" It is not an exaggeration to say that a number of our schools and colleges are presided over by the Devil.

A PLEA FOR VALUE-BASED EDUCATION

Dharma is not only the law of religions; it is a social law; it is the law of humanity; it is the law of the Good. How can education fulfil its purpose without loyalty to the Good?

Therefore, I assert emphatically: we must educate our children, first and foremost, *to know God and to love Him*. The unfortunate thing about most of our schools and colleges today is that God has been divorced from our education. If we make God a reality to our youth, we will surely find that they grow in those true qualities of character without which life has no meaning or significance.

A few decades ago, it was the prevalent fashion among India's youth to deny God. To these young agnostics and atheists, Sadhu Vaswani said, "In a profound sense, God is non-Being, i.e. nothing to the intellect: yet God is Light to the heart, contrite, aspiring and holy. It is to the logical intellect that God is non-Being; but to the heart, rich in intuitions and aspiration, God is the great Reality, God is Light."

This is the great truth that must be emphasised in education — God is Light! Without this awareness, the logical intellect, and the selfish, self-seeking mind will only lead us on the path of materialism, which ends in darkness. But awareness of God, awareness of Light will lead us towards spiritual unfoldment — the highest goal of all education.

As I said to you earlier, our Mira Education believes that the one Light shines in *all* scriptures of all races and religions. The *Vedas*, the *Upanishads* and the Gita are dear to us — as are the New Testament, the *Talmud* and the Holy *Qu'ran*. Our students bow their heads in reverence to the sacred books of Hindus, Christians, Muslims, Parsis, Jains, Buddhists, Jews and Sikhs.

Our ancient system of education was aimed at bringing out the God-in-man. Alas, our current system of education insists on keeping Him out of our learning. That is why education today has become soul-less.

> **20** The real difficulty is that people have no idea of what education is ... We want to provide only such education as would enable the student to earn more. We hardly give any thought to the improvement of character... As long as such ideas persist, there is no hope of our ever knowing the true value of education.
>
> **Mahatma Gandhi**

Let me emphasise one thing: I am not talking about a value-based education for India alone. Training in ethical and spiritual values is, today, a global need.

Today, Management Gurus and Self-Help experts from the West, quote with approval, Mahatma Gandhi's list of Seven Great Blunders that can destroy modern civilisation. Having read these writers, we are waking up to the wisdom of our own great-souled leader. Here is the Mahatma's list of modern social aberrations:

1. Politics without principles
2. Wealth without work
3. Pleasure without conscience
4. Knowledge without character
5. Commerce without morality
6. Worship without sacrifice
7. Science and technology without humanity

I hardly need to tell you – this is exactly what we see around us in the world today. And if this trend is to be reversed, we must educate our youth to respect and uphold those values which make us civilised, cultured, sensitive human beings who can distinguish between good and evil – and make the right moral choices in life.

The sad fact is that most parents and children view education as the highway to a luxurious lifestyle – the elevator that will take them to the penthouse of wealth and affluence. To accomplish this, they will not hesitate to compete ruthlessly with others. The spirit of egotistical competition dominates the high achievers of the younger generation today.

In his 1973 book, *Civilized Man's Eight Deadly Sins*, Konrad Lorenz addresses the following paradox: "All the advantages that man has gained from his ever-deepening understanding of the natural world that surrounds him, his technological, chemical and medical progress, all of which should help to alleviate human suffering... tends instead to favour humanity's destruction ..."

The principle of competition, typical of Western societies, only works towards this, says Lorenz, a distinguished scientist and Nobel Laureate:

"The competition between human beings destroys them with cold and diabolic brutality... Under the pressure of this

A PLEA FOR VALUE-BASED EDUCATION

competitive fury we have not only forgotten what is useful to humanity as a whole, but even that which is good and advantageous to the individual. One asks, which is more damaging to modern humanity: the thirst for money or consuming haste...

Success today, is determined by what the youth perceive as 'status symbols' – the biggest office, the largest salary, the fastest car, the most luxurious holiday ... and so on. Unfortunately, these prestigious acquisitions are also accompanied by the use/abuse of alcohol and drugs, lack of discipline in personal life, with aberrations like divorce, business malpractices and nefarious deals.

Where is the ideal of education as liberation? Where is the dream of education which stands in the service of human freedom?

"Value based education is all very well," a senior educational administrator once told me, "but I wish you could understand that it can't be fitted into our 'required courses' or into our 'credit' system!"

I found that a bewilderingly absurd argument: can we really say that our existing marksheets will not permit us to teach our students to become better human beings?

In his book, *Uncommon Ground,* William Cronon lists ten qualities of a truly educated person. I leave it to you to ask yourself how many 'educated' people today will pass the test:

1. They hear, and they listen.

I am sure that we all hear – but we do not listen, we do not make the effort to understand others.

2. They read.

How many of us today read for the sheer joy of reading? How many young people read in order to improve their minds?

3. They can talk with anyone.

We flatter the rich and powerful; we gossip with friends and family; we 'talk down' to the poor and the lowly. We have forgotten the art of meaningful conversation and thoughtful discussions.

4. They can write.

I am afraid our 'educated' people can only 'text' or 'email'. Writing is forgotten today.

5. They are problem solvers.

We can work at *Sudoku* or crossword puzzles. But we cannot solve the moral, social and ethical problems that face humanity today.

6. They seek truth rigorously.

Modern man's effort is spent in shying away from truth, and in hiding the truth about himself.

7. They are tolerant and humble.

Would you not agree that these qualities are conspicuous by their absence in the 'educated' mass today?

8. They strive to make the world a better place.

I wonder how many of us can put our hands upon our hearts and say honestly, "I have done at least one thing to make this world a better place?"

9. They nurture and empower others.

I am afraid we are overtly obsessed with self-empowerment. We have forgotten that the well-being of all sections of society is crucial to our own happiness.

10. They know the value of 'connecting' with others.

Our achievers know all about making "the right connections". But can they connect with the masses, with the deprived and downtrodden, with people from other races, religions and regions? Do they have the generosity and the friendship to 'connect' with a neighbour who speaks a different language?

---

21 Education, to be complete, must be humane. It must include not only the training of the intellect, but the refinement of the heart and the discipline of the spirit.

Dr. S. Radhakrishnan

A PLEA FOR VALUE-BASED EDUCATION

> **22** The very question—"What does it mean to be a liberally educated person?"—is misleading, deeply so, because it suggests that one can somehow take a group of courses, or accumulate a certain number of credits, or undergo an obligatory set of learning experiences, and emerge liberally educated at the end of the process.
>
> Nothing could be further from the truth. A liberal education is not something any of us ever achieve; it is not a state. Rather, it is a way of living in the face of our own ignorance, a way of groping toward wisdom in full recognition of our own folly, a way of educating ourselves without any illusion that our education will ever be complete.
>
> **William Cronon**

What is the kind of value-based education I would like our students to receive? If you will forgive my saying so, making them pass examinations is not, *should* not be our ultimate aim. I place my emphasis on what I call the *Panchasheel* of education.

> The first is character building
>
> The second is altruistic living
>
> The third is reverence for all life and respect for the great ones of all faiths
>
> The fourth is spiritual unfolding
>
> The fifth is cultivation of the soul

Character, Compassion, Culture and Reverence for all Life: these values capture the ideal of right education. I hope to share with you my views on these ideals in the chapters that follow.

For your Reflection

Do you think our education system nurtures the following qualities?

- Peaceful co-existence with the world of Nature
- Tolerance and sensitivity towards people 'different' from us
- Respect for other cultures and religions
- Pride in our own cultural heritage
- Pride in India and being an Indian
- Respect for all elderly people
- Awareness of Indian traditions and arts
- Respect for teachers
- Care and concern for the welfare of others

In A Lighter Vein...

No Short Cuts

A wealthy businessman was about to enrol his son in a famous university. But he was taken aback when he realised that it would be four years before the boy would be granted his basic degree; and in between, there would be eight semesters with mid-term tests, assignments and exams at the end of each.

Frowning, he flipped through the catalogue of courses and demanded of the Dean, "Why does my son have to go through so many courses? Can't you make the whole thing shorter? I want him to get out of it quickly! He really doesn't need your teaching. He only needs a degree before he takes control of my multimillion dollar business. Do you understand?"

"Certainly, he can take a shorter course," replied the Dean politely. "It all depends on what he wants to make of himself. You see, it takes 20 – 30 years for an oak tree to grow; but a mushroom springs up overnight."

We are all attracted by short-cuts, quick fixes and easy solutions. But, like the oak tree, the mind and character take time to shape up and grow. And we require all eternity to attain to perfection!

FIRST PILLAR OF NEW EDUCATION: CHARACTER BUILDING

The literal meaning of the word 'character' is carving, engraving. Character is that which is to be engraved in the plastic mind of the pupils. New education must sow within them the seeds of character, the seeds of simplicity and service, of purity and prayer.

J.P.Vaswani

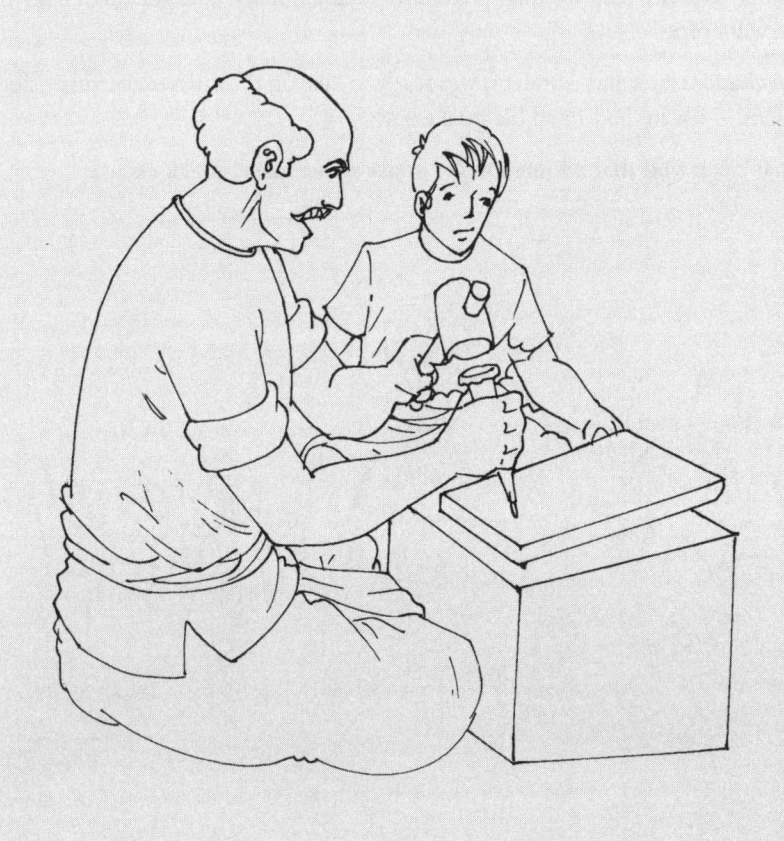

Fix Your Goal

When Abraham Lincoln was a young boy, he worked as a farm labourer, doing heavy, manual work for three days so that he could earn a little money, to pay for a second-hand copy of *The Life Of Washington*. He read the book avidly, and said to a woman he knew, Mrs. Crawford by name: "I don't always intend to do this, you know – delve, grub, husk corn, split rails and the like."

"What do you want to be then?" asked Mrs. Crawford. "I shall be the President," announced Abraham Lincoln. "I shall study and get ready and the chance will come."

The chance came and Abraham was ready to take on the most powerful position in the land – for he had fixed his goal early!

It has been said that winners make goals, while losers make excuses!

First Pillar of New Education: Character Building

A few days before Sadhu Vaswani dropped his physical body, he met a number of young students. One of them said to him, "Beloved Master! Give us a message that we may inscribe in our hearts."

Sadhu Vaswani looked lovingly at the young people and said to them: "Never forget that you and such as you, are the builders of tomorrow. The future is in your hands!"

How true! Our youth represent the future of the country, the future of the world; in them lies the hope for humanity. They will be the builders of a new India, the architects of a new world order.

This was the reason which prompted Sadhu Vaswani to devote himself to the constructive task of cultivating and harnessing youth energy into a positive force. He opened youth centres, and shakti *ashramas* to guide the youth of the land on to the right path.

A few people in America were asked to describe their idea of a well educated person. Here is what some of them had to say:

> A well educated person is a man in a suit who talks with a posh accent. He goes to work with a briefcase, earns good money, lives in a mansion and drives a smart car.

23 New India will be built not in the Assembly or Parliament but in the school and the home...Physical training, social service and the training of the emotions should be regarded as important elements in our educational programmes...

Sadhu Vaswani

NEW EDUCATION CAN MAKE THE WORLD NEW

Galsworthy said, "Character conquers confusion." Today, there is confusion all around us: our minds and hearts are in turmoil. People do not know where to turn for peace and harmony. We have come to realise that money and material comforts do not really make us happy – but we do not know what the alternatives are. All this confusion can be conquered only through the strength and conviction of good character.

If only we are able to produce a generation of men and women of character, we can transform the face of the world, we can change the future of humanity!

> **24** Mental toughness is many things and rather difficult to explain. Its qualities are sacrifice and self-denial. Also, more importantly, it is combined with a perfectly disciplined will that refuses to give in. It's a state of mind — you could call it character in action.
>
> **Vince Lombardi, American Football Coach**

There is so much emphasis on 'professional education' and 'professionalism' in education these days. Every parent wants his/her child to become a successful 'professional'.

Every aspiring student aims high, and dreams of becoming a qualified 'professional' – say a doctor, an engineer, an architect or a software specialist. We look up, with great respect, on 'HR Professionals' 'Management Professionals' and so on and so forth.

Let me ask you – is it not important that *all* these *professionals* including those *professors* who teach them and train them – should, above all *profess* honesty, integrity, truth and idealism? Are not these aspects of character vital to every profession?

Would you trust a corrupt civil engineer to build bridges across our rivers? Would you leave your investments in the hands of a dishonest accountant? Would you consult an unscrupulous, money-minded doctor when you fall ill?

I am sure that your answer to all the above questions is a resounding "No!"

Let me emphasise this: I am not trying to devalue professionalism; I do not wish to denigrate professional education. All I wish to emphasise is that values of character should form the foundation of our educational

FIRST PILLAR OF NEW EDUCATION: CHARACTER BUILDING

> **25** Opportunities are greater today than ever before in our history. Young people graduating from our schools have greater chances for health, happiness and prosperity than had the children of any previous generation. A little money will do more today in setting up a young man or woman in business than it would ever do heretofore. But, there is a greater demand today for people of character than at any time in the history of America. Industry, intelligence, imagination and persistence are great gold mines.
>
> *Roger W. Babson*

- life is larger than livelihood
- the end of knowledge is not just jobs and careers
- the end of knowledge is not gains in silver and gold
- the end of knowledge is service and sacrifice

'Public life' and 'professional career' are terms much bandied about these days. But what people expect from those in public life is probity. What we want from our professionals is honesty and integrity. And what do we come across in real life? 'Cash for votes'. 'Multimillion dollar scandal in banking'. 'Cyber crime fraud'. 'Corruption in defence deals', and so on and so forth!

Am I not right in thinking that if our education system had paid more attention to the cultivation of character, we would have fewer such incidents?

At a Question-Answer Session, a young business executive said to me: "With due respect to the values you speak of, we see all around us that only 'clever' and 'smart' people in the narrowest sense of those words, are able to win over their rivals. If we practise honesty, it does not seem to

system – and serve as the guiding principles of all 'professionals'.

Books could be written on each aspect of good character – such as honesty, integrity, truth and idealism. But all I wish to stress here is that 'professions' should not be reduced to 'means of making more and more money.' Therefore, professional education – indeed, all forms, all types of education should stress the ideas that we have repeatedly discussed in these pages, namely:

pay. Did Sri Krishna not tell Arjuna that he must use all means to win the battle? Is this not what we must also do?"

I must confess to you that I was as much alarmed by the young man's misinterpretation of the message of the Gita, as over his general lack of faith in any value system!

In answer to his question, I explained to him that Sri Krishna does not ask us to do anything and everything to win the battle. He only asks us to work – to do our duty to the best of our ability. But we must realise, that work is not the end, not the goal according to the Gita. Work is only a means to an end; and the end, the goal that Sri Krishna recommends to us – *aatma saakshatkaram* – self-realisation, as the basis for Liberation through surrender to the Lord. To realise this goal, Sri Krishna says, do your duty – but do it as an offering, an *arpanam* to the Lord – and do not be concerned with the results. Leave the results in God's hands.

This is not to be confused with using impure means to achieve our goals!

Ethical confusion arises only when values are not upheld. We live in a world of moral turpitude, because people are only aware of their *rights*, and not of their duties. What the Gita teaches us, in essence, is to do our duty, without expecting anything in return.

---

26 I am afraid many of our students want comfort, ease, enjoyment. I am afraid many of them sleep too much. Too much sleep only dulls the brain. Education is self-discipline. Modern students only run after fashion and folly — after *bhoga*. Students must learn to discipline themselves...

Sadhu Vaswani

27 The spiritual growth from individuality to personality is never achieved by mere intellectual growth ... it is a growth from which issue, as a by-product, moral values, aesthetic sense, ethical awareness with its concern for other individuals, a spirit of service and dedication, and a capacity for team work.

Swami Ranganathananda

FIRST PILLAR OF NEW EDUCATION: CHARACTER BUILDING

Talking about Swami Vivekananda's ideal of Man-Making Education, his devoted disciple, Swami Ranganathananda tells us that human unfoldment must first give us the freedom of *individuality*; but this must eventually evolve into the freedom and responsibility of *personality*. This growth, Swamiji tells us, is something that transcends intellectual dimensions. This is in fact, the way to *atma vikasa* or spiritual unfoldment.

For Your reflection

Watch your thoughts, for they become words.

Watch your words, for they become actions.

Watch your actions, for they become habits.

Watch your habits, for they become character.

Watch your character, for it becomes your destiny.

Author Unknown

In a lighter vein...

Life, Not Words

I recall having read many years ago, concerning an eminent Confucian scholar. He was 80 years of age, and it was believed that no one could equal him in China in learning and understanding.

One day he learnt that far, far away a new doctrine had sprung up that was profoundly deeper than his knowledge. This upset him. He lost his interest in life. He decided that the issue must be decided one way or the other.

He undertook a long journey, traversed many miles and met the master of the new Zen school. He asked him to explain the new doctrine. In answer, the Buddhist monk said to him: "Venerated Sir, the doctrine we propagate is a very simple one. It can be summed up in one sentence: 'To avoid doing evil, to do as much good as possible, this is the teaching of all the Buddhas."

Contd.

NEW EDUCATION CAN MAKE THE WORLD NEW

On hearing this, the old Confucian scholar flared up and said: "What do you mean? I have come here facing the dangers and hazards of a long, perilous journey in spite of my advanced age. And you just quote a little jingle that every three-year-old child knows by heart! Are you mocking at me?"

The Zen master very politely answered: "I am not mocking at you. But please consider that though every three-year-old child knows these words by heart, yet even a man of eighty fails to live up to them!"

SECOND PILLAR OF NEW EDUCATION: COMPASSION

Is there a nobler name and a nobler offering than Compassion – *Maitri?* The modern age, dominated by machinery and materialism, may yet be saved by the spirit of Compassion and Love, which has inspired the noblest philosophers, literatures, arts and idealisms of the East.

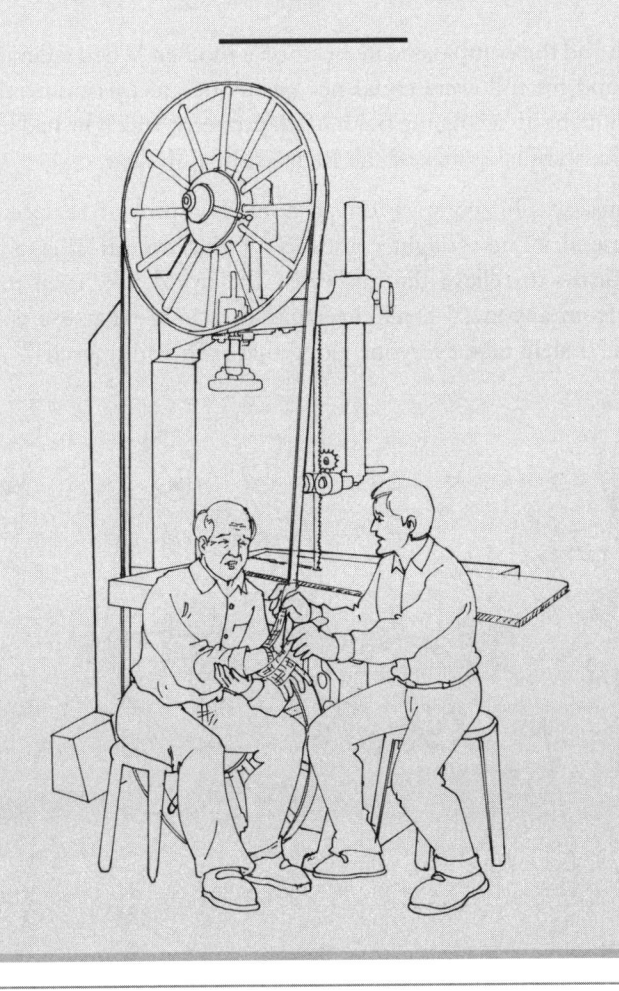

NEW EDUCATION CAN MAKE THE WORLD NEW

Sadhu Vaswani

SWAMIJI'S COMPASSION

Swami Vivekananda put forward the highest concept of service when he coined the term *Daridranarayana* — the Lord in the form of the poor — and asked people to serve Him. "Where would you go to seek God?" he asked. "Are not all the poor, the miserable, the weak, Gods? Why not worship them first?"

Swamiji had the compassionate heart of a mother. When a famine was raging in Bengal and his followers could not get money to carry out relief work, he seriously thought of selling the Belur Math property, which he had just purchased to set up the spiritual centre of the Ramakrishna Mission.

So intense was his compassion, so noble his spirit of service that he once said to a friend, "The thought comes to me that even if I have to undergo a thousand births to relieve the misery of the world, aye, even to remove the least pain from anyone, I shall cheerfully do it. Of what use is my personal *mukti* alone? I shall take everyone along that path with myself!"

Second Pillar of New Education: Compassion

We spoke of character-building, as the first pillar of education; let me emphasise here, that character is built through compassion – through altruistic living, selfless living, *living for others*. Therefore, Sadhu Vaswani urged the youth – Seek not power, seek service!

Here is a beautiful but simple definition of compassion that a friend shared with me: "Compassion is the humane quality of understanding the suffering of others and wanting to do something about it."

Compassion is a sense of *shared* suffering, most often combined with a desire to *alleviate* the suffering, to show special *kindness* to those who suffer. Thus compassion is essentially *empathy*, but with an active slant indicating that the compassionate person will actually seek to aid those they feel for.

Thus, compassion is the foundation for altruistic living, the second mark of a truly educated individual.

I would describe compassion as the crown of all virtues. I believe it is this quality that takes us closest to the Divine within each one of us. When we *practise* – not just feel – this noble virtue, when we go out of ourselves to reach out to others and alleviate their sufferings, we rise to the Highest in us.

There is a parable that tells us of a mother with paralysed arms, who saw her child being swept away along the fast moving currents of a river, but was unable to do anything to save the child. This illustrates the fact that *feeling* is not enough – we have to *act*. Altruistic action is meaningful compassion.

Compassion is love; it is *maitri*, the spirit of friendship, the spirit of caring and sharing. If we fail to inculcate this noble impulse in our students, our education falls short of the best.

Altruistic living is based on the ideal of Universal brotherhood. And who are our brothers? Our brothers and sisters are members of the one family of creation – humans as well

NEW EDUCATION CAN MAKE THE WORLD NEW

as birds and animals. And we need to assert, again and again, "I am my brother's keeper!"

If I had a million tongues, I would appeal to my young friends who are going to be tomorrow's leaders and opinion makers – Seek not power! Seek service!

Let us do as much good as we can, in as many ways as we can, on as many occasions as we can, and as long as we can!

"What do we live for if not to make the world less difficult for each other?" asks the famous writer and novelist, George Eliot. I am afraid our career-oriented, job-driven education is making our youth self-centred, constricting them to lead narrow, selfish lives. But it is only in compassionate, altruistic living that we can discover the best that we are capable of.

Therefore, let me say to my young friends: give of yourself, give of your time, talents and energies to lighten the loads of the weary and the heavy-laden!

Albert Schweitzer was always pained to hear people say, "If only I were rich, I would do great things to

> **28** The essential distinction between savages and civilised men lies not in differences of dress, dwelling, food, deportment or possessions – but in the way we treat our fellow human beings. It is the degree of humanity in our relationship with others that decides how far we have travelled from a state of savagery towards an ideal world of civilised beings who truly have learnt the art of peaceful coexistence.
>
> *Aung San Syu Kyi*

SECOND PILLAR OF NEW EDUCATION: COMPASSION

help and serve others." He would promptly point out to them that all of us could be *rich* in love, generosity and compassion; and that we could always extend our loving care and compassion to others. This, he said, was worth more than all the money in the world!

> **29** No man is so poor as to have nothing worth giving; as well might mountain streamlets say they have nothing to give the sea, because they are not rivers! Give what you have. To someone, it may be better than you dare to think!
>
> *H.W. Longfellow*

Can you read? Then read to a blind student. Can you write? Then write a letter, fill a form for someone who is not so lucky as you are. If you are not very hungry, share your food with someone who is. If you are at peace with yourself, reach out to those who are in pain, and disturbed by their suffering.

All of us have something to give! Let us give what we can to others – our time, our talent and know-how, our effort, our understanding, our love, our concern, our sympathy, our smiles. Let us give with love and compassion.

Sadhu Vaswani believed that the root of true education is reverence and its fruit is service – service of the poor and broken ones, the lonely and the lost.

Our students are taught Civics to make them responsible citizens. They learn that they must pay their bills and taxes on time. They are told that they must exercise their franchise and fulfill their democratic duties. They are taught to obey all traffic rules; they are taught never to break the laws of the land . . .

But this is not enough! Doing our duty is alright – but we need to do our duty *and a little more!* Therefore our students must grow beyond responsible citizenship to become good human beings. They must realise that the opposite of love is not hatred, but *apathy* or indifference – indifference, insensitivity to the needs of others.

> **30** It may seem to you conceited to suppose that you can do anything important towards improving the lot of mankind. But this is a fallacy. You must believe that you can help bring about a better world! A good society is produced only by good *individuals*.
>
> *Bertrand Russel*

NEW EDUCATION CAN MAKE THE WORLD NEW

Even if one person is comforted by your words; even if one person's broken heart is healed by your understanding; even if someone's misery is wiped out by your kindness – you have made a difference! Your education has served its purpose!

May I tell you, I believe that altruistic living, a life filled with compassion, is the Life Beautiful, the Life Spiritual. It was a true saint of God who said: Prayer without work is as bad as work without prayer!

There is a simple question that all wise men ask us: How can we claim that we love God, if we do not love His children, our fellow human beings? How can we claim to be truly educated, if there is no compassion, no sensitivity in us for the sufferings and struggles of our fellow human beings?

Don't hold back! Don't underestimate yourself and your capacity to give! Don't ever imagine that you cannot make a difference! We may feel that our effort is but a drop in the ocean – but every little drop counts in the ocean that is life!

Every educated individual should be aware of this great truth – to live is to give! The more you give to others, the more you live; but if you do not give of yourself in compassion and altruism, you are no better than a dead person!

---

31 **O child of Beloved Bharata! Look around you and see that the world is sad, is broken, is torn with tragedy, is smitten with suffering. Living in such a world, you must learn to share the good things of life that have been bestowed upon you; you must share them with those that are in need. Remember, you cannot be happy when so many around you are unhappy. If you would be happy, go and make others happy. The happiness that you give to others will come back to you, such is the law. For happiness moves in a circle.**

Sadhu Vaswani

SECOND PILLAR OF NEW EDUCATION: COMPASSION

For Your Reflection

Compassion is an attribute of the Divine in all of us.

Compassion is . . . awareness of the One-in-all.

Compassion is . . . the key to peace and harmony in society.

Compassion is . . . tender love combined with emotional strength to do good to others.

Compassion is . . . unconditional, undemanding, unforced.

Compassion is . . . forgiveness.

Compassion is . . . oneness.

Compassion is . . . goodness.

Compassion is . . . caring and sharing.

Compassion is . . . Love-in-action.

In A Lighter Vein . . .

The distinguished American author and lecturer, Leo Buscaglia, once talked about a contest he was asked to judge. The purpose of the contest was to find the most caring child. The winner was a four-year-old child whose next-door neighbour was an elderly gentleman who had recently lost his wife. Upon seeing the man cry, the little boy went into the old gentleman's yard, climbed onto his lap, and just sat there. When his mother asked him what he had said to the neighbour, the little boy said, "Nothing, I just helped him cry."

THIRD PILLAR OF NEW EDUCATION: CULTURE

Book knowledge stays in the head: Culture flows into life. Book knowledge is heavy: Culture gives understanding and so reduces the friction of life. Culture weaves understanding and gentleness into actual living.

Sadhu Vaswani

THIRD PILLAR OF NEW EDUCATION: CULTURE

Charity With Courtesy

A little boy was walking down the Rue Royale in Paris with his grandfather, who was a kind and courteous gentleman. They passed by a blind man, who was seated on a low stool, begging for alms. The grandfather gave four coins to the boy and asked him to put it in the blind man's hat.

The boy dropped the coins into the hat and resumed his walk. "You must touch your hat before the gentleman," his grandfather suggested, mildly.

"Why should I do that?" asked the little boy.

"One should always do it when one is giving alms," the grandfather replied. "It shows your culture and good manners."

"But this man is blind," persisted the boy. "He can't even see me touch my hat for him."

"He may even be a fraud," said the grandfather. "But you still have to show him courtesy."

The grandfather was a man of culture.

Third Pillar of New Education: Culture

The word "culture" is used today by sociologists, anthropologists and even management experts, in its different connotations. Some marketing professionals even identify culture in terms of consumption and consumer goods (as in high culture, low culture, folk culture, or popular culture).

More recently, the United Nations Educational, Scientific and Cultural Organisation (Unesco) (2002) described culture as follows: "... culture should be regarded as the set of distinctive spiritual, material, intellectual and emotional features of society or a social group, and that it encompasses, in addition to art and literature, lifestyles, ways of living together, value systems, traditions and beliefs".

> **32** Do you wish to build universities in India? Then understand a little, of the great legacy that is yours as children of India, as children of this ancient land. Great is your heritage: great is your inheritance.
>
> *Sadhu Vaswani*

DICTIONARY DEFINITIONS OF CULTURE

- Culture refers to the cumulative deposit of knowledge, experience, beliefs, values, attitudes, meanings, hierarchies, religion, notions of time, roles, spatial relations, concepts of the universe, and material objects and possessions acquired by a group of people in the course of generations through individual and group striving.

- Culture in its broadest sense is cultivated behaviour; that is the totality of a person's learned, accumulated experience which is socially transmitted, or more briefly, behaviour through social learning.

- Culture is the sum total of the learned behaviour of a group of people that are generally considered to be the tradition of that people and are transmitted from generation to generation.

Let me tell you right at the outset, that I am no theorist, who can offer you a comprehensive definition of culture!

THIRD PILLAR OF NEW EDUCATION: CULTURE

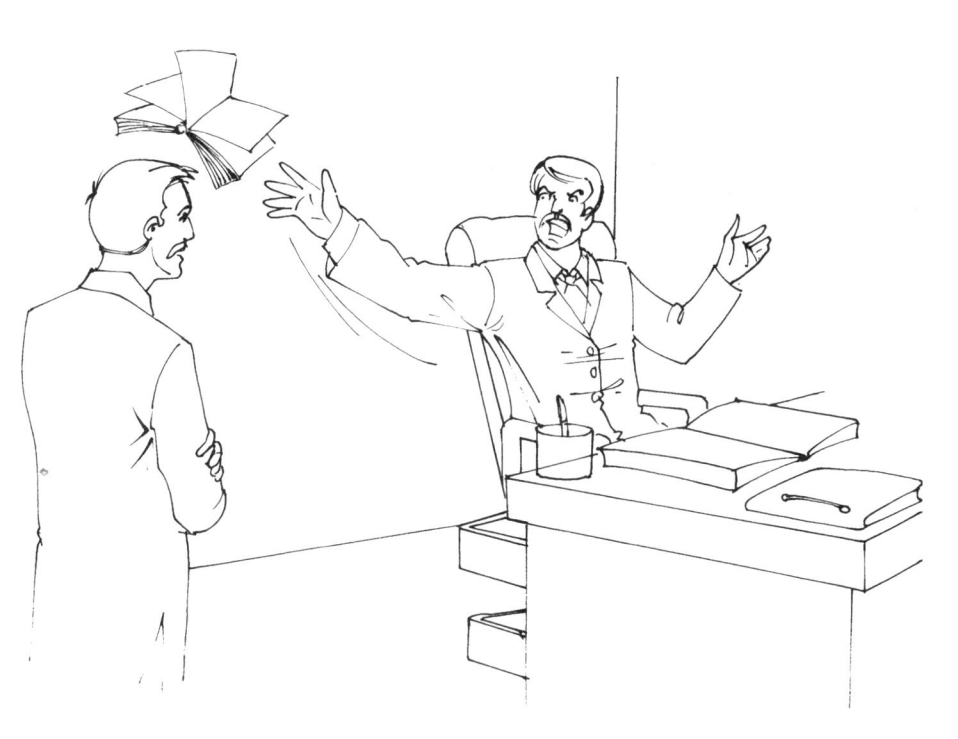

But my association with my Beloved Master has taught me many things about what he regarded as true culture.

Sadhu Vaswani said to us, "No one is truly cultured who does not show courtesy to those whom accident of birth has made his 'inferiors' – to the poor, the needy, the neglected and the weak!"

He added, "Call him not cultured who speaks harshly to his servants."

I learnt this from Mahatma Gandhi, the great-souled one – that true culture could be cultivated by disciplining desires and emotions. Self-discipline and self-control are the key to understanding the culture that is unique to the land of the Vedas.

Western culture lays emphasis on power and material acquisitions; it is the essence of Indian culture to value the spirit – the eternal, imperishable *atman*– above all else. This is why you will find common people bowing to leaders, millionaires, celebrities in the West, while in India, leaders, millionaires and common public alike bow down in reverence to men and women who have renounced the world and live a life of contemplation and reflection.

Sadhu Vaswani described the Bhagavad Gita as "a Text Book of Culture". He would often refer to the Second Chapter of the Gita which gives us a pen-picture of the model man of culture. This is the portrait of the *stita pragna* – the man of balance, who is stable of mind, steadfast, 'freed from passion, fear and anger', yet full of love in his heart – love for the Lord and His Creation. The man of Culture is a man of Light and Love.

The Buddha too, was a man of culture. His philosophy is expressed in the following words:

"I plough and sow; and from my ploughing and sowing I rear immortal fruit. My field is Religion. The weed I pluck up are passions. My plough is wisdom. My seed is purity."

What a glorious vision of culture is given to us in these lines!

Both Swami Vivekananda and Sadhu Vaswani believed that it was through new education that a renaissance would be ushered in India. They were convinced that this Indian Renaissance would be essentially a spiritual awakening, a spiritual unfolding.

Arnold Toynbee, the distinguished historian, once observed that the history of Western thought in the Nineteenth Century, replaced religion with technology, as the centre of interest. But he also prophesied that this movement would be reversed in the twenty-first century, in which men would turn back from technology to religion.

I do not know what my readers will make of this prediction: but I have no doubt in my mind that we are fast approaching an age when values of character will be regarded as far superior to technological advancement.

The youth are, by nature, attracted to hero-worship. In the absence of worthy role models, they turn to celebrities, film stars and political leaders. When they have *mahatmas* and great souls to follow, they will surely learn to worship high ideals. And this is what we need today – our students

THIRD PILLAR OF NEW EDUCATION: CULTURE

must be taught devotion to the great saints and heroes of humanity, devotion to the great ideals of service and sacrifice.

Such idealism can be a true source of inspiration to the youth. Our new education should aim at awakening this consciousness. Youth, as Sadhu Vaswani emphasised, is hope, not despair. And if India is to be rebuilt for glory and supremacy, we need young people, filled with hope and faith and courage, to lay the spiritual foundation of a new nation.

Education of the best type has as its objective, the health and happiness of the whole man. The heart, the mind, the will and the senses must be purified, so that the *atman* is restored to its original strength.

When the whole man is purified, strengthened, enriched and illumined, the youth of the country, imbued with tremendous idealism, will be ready to lay the foundation of a new Indian nation.

Is it not true that the current system of education has not helped our students to recognise and appreciate Indian culture? They know all about the culture of globalisation, and the industrial/ technological culture of the West. But how many of them are genuinely interested in Indian culture? How many of them realise that it can enrich the thought and life of the world as a whole?

When our young people are educated in the spirit of the true Indian culture, they will take pride in being Indian. They will turn their back on the slavish habit of imitation. In fact, Sadhu Vaswani taught us that slavishness, imitation, intolerance, aggressiveness, narrowness and coarseness are sins against culture. While inner independence, simplicity, refinement, large-mindedness, humility, free activity, rich vital idealism – are all true marks of a cultured individual.

> **33** The ideal man of India is not the magnanimous man of Greece or the valiant knight of medieval Europe, but the free man of the spirit, who has attained insight into the Universe by rigid discipline and practice of disinterested virtues, who has freed himself from the prejudices of his time and place.
>
> **Dr. S. Radhakrishnan**

NEW EDUCATION CAN MAKE THE WORLD NEW

Man becomes what he thinks, taught our ancient *rishis*. Therefore it is not theory, not a set of definitions and maxims, but exemplary role-models, great figures who can shape the lives of the students. And India has given us so many of these great souls, radiant with the light of lofty ideals – rishis and sages, poets and prophets, heroes and holy men, singers of the spirit, men of action and devotion, men and women of dedicated lives – from Yagnavalkya, Sukha, Maitreyi and Arjuna, to the later ones, Buddha and Mahavira, Kabir and Guru Nanak and Guru Gobind Singh, Chatrapati Shivaji, Lokamanya Tilak, Ramakrishna Paramahansa, Swami Vivekananda, Mahatma Gandhi and Sadhu Vaswani.

If there is one thing above all else that Indian culture emphasises, it is the unity of the Self, the unity of the *Atman*. The call of India, the call of Sri Krishna to us is this: "Awaken the soul! Dedicate thy *shakti* to India and humanity!" This was the message of our ancient rishis, our deathless scriptures: "Cultivate the Soul!"

For Your Reflection

At a time when moral aggression is compelling people to capitulate to queer ways of life, when vast experiments in social structure and political organisation are being made at enormous cost of life and suffering, when we stand perplexed and confused before the future with no clear light to guide our way, the power of the human soul is the only refuge. If we resolve to be governed by it, our civilisation may enter upon its most glorious epoch... There are many 'dissatisfied children of the spirit of the West', to use Romain Rolland's phrase, who are oppressed that the universality of her great thoughts has been defamed for ends of violent action, that they are trapped in a blind alley and are savagely crushing each other out of existence. When an old binding culture is being broken, when ethical standards are dissolving, when we are being aroused out of apathy or awakened out of unconsciousness, when there is in the air general fermant, inward stirring, cultural crisis, then a high tide of spiritual agitation sweeps over people and we sense in the horizon something novel, something unprecedented, the beginning of a spiritual renaissance.

– *Dr. S. Radhakrishnan*

THIRD PILLAR OF NEW EDUCATION: CULTURE

IN A LIGHTER VEIN...

THERE'S A FINE TO BE PAID

La Guardia was a famous and distinguished statesman. He was a former mayor of New York. Many of you will know that one of the airports of New Jersey is named after him.

Once, he was presiding over a police court, when a trembling, old man was brought before him. His offence was that he had stolen a loaf of bread, for his family was starving.

La Guardia heard the policeman state the case. Then he turned to the old man. "I have to punish you," he told the old man. "The law has to take its course, and it makes no exceptions. I have to sentence you to a fine of ten dollars!"

Ten dollars! The old man was dumbfounded. He did not even possess ten cents!

Impassive as ever, La Guardia continued, "As the ten dollars is to be paid immediately, I give you the amount myself." Reaching into his pocket, he withdrew a ten-dollar bill, which he dropped into the collection box. "And now I remit the fine."

Turning to the large audience who were staring at him with gaping mouths, he continued, "Furthermore, I am going to fine everybody in this courtroom fifty cents - for living in a town where a man had to steal bread in order to eat."

With those words, he ordered his bailiff to collect the fine of fifty cents from each and every one of the onlookers. A hat was passed round and the sum collected - $47.50 - was handed over to the old man, who left the court - free and happy!

La Guardia was not only a statesman and a highly regarded public figure: he was a truly cultured man.

FOURTH PILLAR OF NEW EDUCATION : REVERENCE FOR ALL LIFE

Reverence is the secret of true education . . . And this, as the great poet, Goethe said: Reverence is of three types – reverence for what is above us, for what is beneath us and for what is around us.

J. P. Vaswani

FOURTH PILLAR OF NEW EDUCATION : REVERENCE FOR ALL LIFE

You Cannot Kill Your Conscience!

This is a true story. The incident happened in the US a few years ago.

Miss X was a teacher in a High School. A strict teacher, a no-nonsense person and a firm disciplinarian. Miss X was valued by the school authorities, as she was one of the few staff members who could control disruptive students. As for the pupils, a few of them respected her for the values she passed on to them; most of them were afraid of her; and some of them hated her, because they could not fool around or do as they pleased in her class.

Some students belonging to this latter group hatched an evil plot against her, after she had failed them in a test. It was quite another matter that none of them really deserved to pass; in their vicious anger, they decided to 'punish' the teacher who had dared to stand up against their misdemeanors. Five of them (including a girl) decided to poison her.

They knew Miss X was in the habit of relaxing with a cup of coffee during the brief recess between classes. They managed to get hold of some deadly potassium cyanide, which they added to her coffee.

When Miss X was about to drink the coffee – the cup was almost at her lips – the girl rushed towards her and knocked the cup off her teacher's hands. Sobbing uncontrollably, she confessed that she and her friends had laced the coffee with cyanide, but she could not allow the teacher to be killed. Her conscience had overwhelmed her – even if it was only at the last moment! The girl had been part of the plot to kill the teacher. But it was only a qualm of conscience that enabled her to save the teacher's life!

Fourth Pillar of New Education: Reverence For All Life

It was the poet Tennyson who penned those memorable lines, which I love to quote again and again:

> Let knowledge grow from more to more,
>
> But more of reverence in us dwell!

If there is one quality which is sadly lacking in our lives today, it is the beautiful virtue of reverence: reverence for what is above us, reverence for what is around us, and reverence for what is beneath us.

Gurudev Sadhu Vaswani emphasised the thought that education should be imparted – and imbibed – in the spirit of a *yagna* to the Lord. Our sports, our games, our literary activities, our scientific experiments and all our curricular and extra-curricular activities, would not be fruitful, he said, until they were offered as a *yagna* – a sacrifice – to the Lord.

Vidya dadati vinayam – so our scriptures teach us. True knowledge, true scholarship is humility. As I have pointed out earlier, current education has only succeeded in making our students sharp and shrewd. They become clever, aggressive and competitive; they are motivated only by self-interest; this is something that needs to be changed.

Education must be rooted in one form of fundamental reverence: reverence for the teacher; and on the part of the teacher, respect and love for the pupils. Such was the spirit that prevailed in our ancient *ashramas*. How I wish we could rekindle this beautiful attitude today!

If there is such a thing as transforming power in education, you will not find it in the text books; you will find it in the teacher. Clever men and women can be found everywhere; but what good education needs are teachers of the true type – teachers who can be friends and guardians of their young students – teachers who can inspire trust and respect in their students. Only in such an atmosphere

FOURTH PILLAR OF NEW EDUCATION : REVERENCE FOR ALL LIFE

of mutual respect can values can be imparted.

In the Gita, we have what is essentially a *samvada* – a dialogue between Arjuna and Krishna. True education is essentially a dialogue between the teacher and the pupil; it is a communion of their minds and hearts.

We must encourage our students to respect all races and religions. The world today is being torn apart by religious fundamentalism and religious fanaticism. Our students must learn that true religion is not institutional, that true religion will never condone violence and hatred.

We must teach our students to have reverence and respect for Indian ideals – but, at the same time, we should also teach them that truly great Ones are not a monopoly of India, but have appeared in all countries and all climes; they have enriched the lives of all races, and inspired and illumined all religions.

Therefore, let our students love and revere Sri Rama and Sri Krishna; Allah and Isa; Mahavira, Buddha, Zoroaster and Guru Nanak. Let them be taught of Veda Vyasa, Vashishta; Prophet Mohammed and St. Francis;

34 An inner revolution, I think, of the individual, is the prime necessity of India. So we start with the student, aiming at an inner revolution of his life. The inner first: the outer will come as an inevitable expression of the inner. Awaken the divine spark within the student, and you will light a fire which no outer coercion can quench.

Sadhu Vaswani

Guru Gobind Singh and Baha'u'llah; Sri Ramakrishna and Mahatma Gandhi.

The inner revolution – the cultivation of the spirit – in our students, must come from the teachings of these great ones from East and West.

Reverence is also required for the world around us – the world of Nature. Today, I am told, 'Environmental Science' has become a 'compulsory subject' for the graduates of all disciplines in a few Indian Universities. But I feel that theory is not enough. Our students must be taught to revere, and be one with the spirit of Nature!

Today, it seems to me, man is at *war* with nature! He has exploited the soil; he has destroyed the habitat of wild animals; he has polluted the seas and rivers and degraded the very environment in which he dwells.

> May peace prevail in the skies
>
> May peace prevail on earth
>
> May peace prevail in vast space
>
> May peace prevail in the flowing river,
>
> And in plants and trees!
>
> *Atharva Veda*

Man, they say, is the Crown of God's creation. Therefore, let our students be taught to take on the role of guardians, protectors and wardens of Nature!

Reverence for Nature is essential – for this alone will help future generations to survive upon this planet. Our children must be taught to revere, preserve and protect this blessed earth – for the sake of their children, and their children's children!

True, our students need knowledge, specialisation in key disciplines, practical application and leadership skills. But they must also be taught to love, revere and pour out their compassion on the creatures of God, who suffer and groan in pain.

Sometime ago, one of India's distinguished and valiant daughters, Dr. Kiran Bedi, I.P.S., visited our Sadhu Vaswani Mission to address a special gathering of teachers that we had organised in connection with the Platinum Jubilee of our MIRA Movement in Education. Asked about the kind of educational reforms we needed in India, she asserted boldly that community service of the deprived and downtrodden should be given equal, if not more importance

FOURTH PILLAR OF NEW EDUCATION : REVERENCE FOR ALL LIFE

than theoretical education in our colleges and universities.

Sadhu Vaswani would have rejoiced in spirit, to hear her repeat the ideal that he cherished dearly – service of the poor, service to society. He urged the MIRA students to serve not only the poor and needy, the sick and the suffering ones – but also to serve the criminals and sinners. To this day, our students and youth groups visit the inmates of the local jail on *Rakshabhandan* day, and tie *Rakhis* on the wrists of their brothers, the prisoners. They visit the prison during Diwali to distribute sweets and new clothes.

Reverence for what is beneath us is vital. Therefore, we should emphasise the need to put an end to all forms of exploitation. Our students must be taught that all our transactions, all our relationships, all our activities, should be based on the principle of justice.

Of course, even corporates and multinationals today are raising their

---

36 To every student, I say: "Take Sri Krishna at His word!" Does He not say that the dearest Name for Him is *Daridra Narayana* – the Lord of the poor and needy ones? So see Him in the poor, and seeing Him, make your knowledge an instrument of service, your education an offering, a *yagna* to the Lord!

— **Sadhu Vaswani**

NEW EDUCATION CAN MAKE THE WORLD NEW

voices against all other forms of exploitation. So I might be forgiven for voicing my support for birds and animals – those dumb, defenceless creatures, which Sadhu Vaswani taught us, are our *younger brothers and sisters* in the One family of creation.

Our students are eloquent in debates over child labour, racial intolerance, and injustice against the working classes. All forms of exploitation must cease. But can we be silent on the subject of animal welfare and animal rights?

Animals have no press, no TV, no media, no spokesperson to voice their grievances. They need friends and supporters; they need articulate spokespersons. Our students should be encouraged to take on this challenging role!

And let me emphasise this again – animal welfare is not enough! We must speak of animal rights! Men have their rights; have animals no rights? The time has come for the younger generation to stand up and be counted for the inviolability of the right to life – both human and non-human.

Reverence for the vast universe that God created; reverence for the great ones of humanity; reverence for the poor and needy; reverence for the speechless world of birds and beasts – this is what will enable our students to be liberated from the vain and empty cult of the ego – and this, our Education must aim to achieve. For true liberation is emancipation from the ego; and I repeat these beautiful words from our scriptures: *Ya vidya sa vimuktyate* – that is true knowledge, which liberates us!

Let me end, with the beautiful words of my Beloved Gurudeva:

Leaving aside the cult of the ego, we pass on to the welfare of the community. From the love of the community, we needs must rise to the love of the Motherland ...We must rise yet higher: we must learn to serve Humanity. Yet higher still: we must learn to serve all creatures and all creation, and so enrich our lives with the treasure of compassion ...Yet higher must we rise to the love of the Spirit, love of God, love of the life Universal.

37

Holy, holy, holy is every creature. Touch ye these children of the Lord with reverence and love! Harm them not! But serve them in deep humility! These birds and beasts, these creatures, children of Krishna, are the forms the Lord hath put on!

Sadhu Vaswani

FOURTH PILLAR OF NEW EDUCATION : REVERENCE FOR ALL LIFE

In A Lighter Vein...

Book of Noble Conduct

St. Serapio of Egypt was a learned one who bore witness to the great precept of the religion of service in deeds of daily living. Like most 'scholars' of those days, he was very, very poor. His education and learning had not been used to advance his status and wealth in society. His most valuable raiment was a long coat of very coarse cloth, which he often pawned, and once sold outright to help the poor and needy. At times, he would even pawn himself — commit himself to prolonged manual labour for a certain period of time, working for a rich man — so that he could obtain money to feed the poor.

One of his close friends was shocked to see him in tattered clothes, on one occasion. "What is the matter?" he remonstrated. "Why are you so famished and unclothed?"

"The answer to that question is to be realised – not interrogated," was the saint's reply. "I cannot bear to see helpless ones suffer. My *Book of Noble Conduct* tells me that I must sell off all my belongings to serve the poor and the needy."

"May I see this *Book of Noble Conduct* which you regard so highly?" enquired the friend.

"That book has also been sold off to help my needy friends,". the saint replied briskly. "It was sold for a noble purpose — and it will pay doubly, because the person who obtains it will be transformed by the spirit of service, and do all he can to help the desolate and destitute."

He was a great man imbued with reverence for all humanity!

Other Books and Booklets By Dada J.P. Vaswani

In English:
10 Commandments of A Successful Marriage
108 Pearls of Practical Wisdom
108 Simple Prayers of A Simple Man
108 Thoughts on Success
114 Thoughts on Love
A Little Book of Life
A Simple And Easy Way To God
A Treasure of Quotes
Around The Camp Fire
Begin The Day With God
Bhagavad Gita in a Nutshell
Burn Anger Before Anger Burns You
Daily Inspiration
Daily Inspiration (Booklet)
Destination Happiness
Dewdrops of Love
Does God Have Favourites?
Ecstasy and Experiences
Formula For Prosperity
Gateways to Heaven
God In Quest of Man
Good Parenting
Gurukul
Gurukul II
How To Overcome Depression
I am a Sindhi
In 2012 All Will Be Well
Joy Peace Pills
Kill Fear Before Fear Kills You
Ladder of Abhyasa
Lessons Life Has Taught Me
Life After Death
Management Moment by Moment
Mantras For Peace Of Mind
Many Paths: One Goal
Nearer, My God, To Thee!
Peace or Perish
Positive Power of Thanksgiving
Questions Answered
Sadhu Vaswani : His Life And Teachings
Saints For You and Me
Saints With A Difference
Secrets of Health And Happiness
Shake Hand With Life
Short Sketches of Saints Known & Unknown
Sketches of Saints Known & Unknown
Stop Complaining: Start Thanking!
Swallow Irritation Before Irritation Swallows You
Teachers are Sculptors
The Goal Of Life and How To Attain It
The Little Book of Freedom From Stress
The Little Book of Prayer
The Little Book of Service
The Little Book of Success
The Little Book of Wisdom
The Little Book of Yoga
The Magic of Forgiveness
The Perfect Relationship: Guru and Disciple
The Seven Commandments of the Bhagavad Gita
The Terror Within
The Way of Abhyasa (How To Meditate)
Thus Have I Been Taught
Tips For Teenagers
What You Would Like To know About Karma
What You Would Like To know About Hinduism

What To Do When Difficulties Strike
Why Do Good People Suffer?
You Are Not Alone God Is With You!

Story Books:
101 Stories For You And Me
25 Stories For Children and also for Teens
It's All A Matter of Attitude
Snacks For The Soul
More Snacks For The Soul
Break The Habit
The Lord Provides
The Heart of a Mother
The King of Kings
The One Thing Needful
The Patience of Purna
The Power of Good Deeds
The Power of Thought
Trust Me All in All or Not at All
Whom Do You Love the Most
You Can Make A Difference

In Hindi:
Aalwar Santon Ki Mahan Gaathaayen
Atmik Jalpaan
Aapkay Karm, Aapkaa Bhaagy Banaatay Hein
Atmik Poshan
Bhakton Ki Uljhanon Kaa Saral Upaai
Bhale Logon Ke Saath Bura Kyon?
Dainik Prerna
Dar Se Mukti Paayen
Ishwar Tujhe Pranam
Jiski Jholi Mein Hain Pyaar
Krodh Ko Jalayen Swayam Ko Nahin
Laghu Kathayein
Mrutyu Hai Dwar... Phir Kya?
Nava Pushp (Bhajans In Hindi and Sindhi)
Prarthna ki Shakti
Pyar Ka Masiha
Sadhu Vaswani: Unkaa Jeevan Aur Shikshaayen
Safal Vivah Ke Dus Rahasya
Santon Ki Leela
Sri Bhagavad Gita: Gaagar Mein Saagar

In Marathi:
Krodhala Shaanth Kara, Krodhane Ghala Ghalnya Purvee (Burn Anger Before Anger Burns You)
Jiski Jholi Mein Hain Pyaar
Life After Death
Pilgrim of Love
Sind and the Sindhis
Sufi Sant (Sufi Saints of East and West)
What You Would Like To Know About Karma

Other Publications:

Recipe Books:
90 Vegetarian Sindhi Recipes
Di-li-cious Vegetarian Recipes
Simply Vegetarian

Books on Dada J. P. Vaswani:
A Pilgrim of Love
Dada J.P. Vaswani: His Life and Teachings
Dada J.P. Vaswani's Historic Visit to Sind
Dost Thou Keep Memory
How To Embrace Pain
Living Legend
Moments with a Master